Clare, A Light in the Garden

Revised and Expanded

Murray Bodo

Clare

A LIGHT IN
THE GARDEN

Revised and Expanded

ST. ANTHONY MESSENGER PRESS

CINCINNATI, OHIO

Nihil Obstat: Rev. Thomas Richstatter, O.F.M., S.T.D.
Rev. Edward J. Gratsch

Imprimi Potest: Rev. John Bok, O.F.M.
Provincial

Imprimatur: +James H. Garland, V.G.
Archdiocese of Cincinnati
April 16, 1992

Cover design, book design and illustrations by Julie Lonneman
ISBN 0-86716-122-1

She was the first flower

in Francis' garden,

and she shone like a radiant star,

fragrant as a flower blossoming

white and pure in springtime.

—St. Bonaventure

In memory of my mother

Pauline Bodo

1913-1989
  quiet love
    courage

Contents

Foreword to
Clare, A Light in the Garden

1979 EDITION

T he first biographer of Clare, Thomas of Celano, began his work in 1255, soon after her canonization, and completed it the following year. Celano's *The Legend of St. Clare of Assisi* draws heavily upon the canonical process and document of canonization and the testimony of eyewitnesses to the life and sanctity of Clare. It is a small volume, but it zeroes in on the essential elements of her life.

Since then other books have been written about Clare's life, her spirituality and the nature of her contemplation. This book is not that kind of book. It pretends to be neither a biography nor a spiritual meditation on Clare's life. Nor is it a portrayal of the life of the Poor Clares. It is a story based upon Clare's relationship with Francis of Assisi. Their friendship opened my imagination to a whole new dimension of story.

This is that story as I discovered it visiting the places dear to Clare and Francis, and writing down the thoughts that came to me on my journey. Because the book is largely an account of the part Francis played in Clare's life and she in his, it is a story of intimacy, but an intimacy of mystery and space. Clare and Francis reverenced the mystery in each other and allowed enough space between them to preserve that mystery.

The story is not necessarily always factual, but to me it is true. And if you believe, as I do, that the imagination sometimes brings us closer to truth than does fact, then perhaps you can dare to believe that the imagination can also remember something history has failed to record.

Murray Bodo, O.F.M.
Casa Papa Giovanni
Assisi, 1979

Foreword to the Revised Edition

Mouvance is the name of the process whereby texts in a manuscript tradition change with each new copying. Sometimes this is due to scribal error; sometimes it is the result of glosses the scribes themselves make, in effect rewriting the text as they read and copy it. A scribe's gloss, then, can be either an error, an explanation, or in some cases a manipulation of the very text the scribe is copying. Add to this conscious harassment of the text the fact that in the Middle Ages authors do not always make exclusive claims for their texts. Sometimes they write multiple versions of the same text; sometimes they borrow whole sections of other works.

Having written *Clare, A Light in the Garden* almost fifteen years ago, it is now a more objective text for me, though I still remember having the feelings and thoughts that I read there today. And so, in rewriting this book, I felt like a medieval scribe copying and making glosses on my own text, not in order to subvert that text, but like a jazz musician, to improvise on its principal motifs in order to incorporate additional insights that I hope broaden and deepen the image of St. Clare which rose like a melody in my imagination some fifteen years ago. These new insights have revealed themselves to me only slowly as I came to know St. Clare more intimately through prayer and study and through dialogue with those whose living of her Rule of Life make St. Clare a real, dynamic presence even today, eight hundred years after her birth.

I've had the luxury to preserve what still rings true to my original insight and at the same time to modulate parts of the text, thereby denying the original text any claim to being *the* authoritative text of authorial intention. In the process I've found myself wishing the text could be repeatedly copied by hand like a medieval manuscript, so that this present rewriting, too, would be denied canonicity; and each new copying would incorporate the creativity of the individual scribe. The text in the meantime would become a communal effort with more and more minds and hearts at work in its writing.

I do wish, in fact, that each reader could rewrite the text in the reading, which is, as a matter of fact, what happens when any text is read. But we are in the age of printing, and I realize this is probably the last re-copying this text will know. Therefore, I've tried to incorporate all the glosses my own reading of the text occasioned, from the first time I read the printed text to the time of this last reading that precipitated the glosses that become now this new edition of *Clare, A Light in the Garden*.

The year 1979 was the first time I read the printed text of *Clare, A Light in the Garden*. On finishing the reading, I wrote a letter to myself, which is the first gloss I put on the text. This is what I wrote:

And so what is the ending is only the beginning. I have written of Francis and Clare, but the story of God and Clare is yet to be written. That story far surpasses this one in its intensity, its ardor and fidelity, and only a contemplative can write it. Perhaps it cannot be written because it is a hidden story, the story of the union of a great soul with her God.

Clare's life with God lies deep within, and no one knows that story but God. But I do know that someone with Clare's capacity for human love and fidelity must surely penetrate the heavens when that love is directed to the All-Good God. I believe our love for one another is the only reliable measure of our love for God. Clare's pure love for Francis and his Dream is for me the perfect analogue of her love for God.

The real story of Clare is the mystery of the light within her soul, the rose within the rose. It is, as the poet T. S. Eliot wrote,

A condition of complete simplicity
(Costing not less than everything)
...
When the tongues of flame are in-folded
Into the crowned knot of fire
And the fire and the rose are one.
—*Little Gidding*[1]

The following text represents all the glosses I've made upon the text from 1979 to 1991 when I submitted these emendations, deletions and additions for publication. The real story of Clare still evades me as all mystery must evade us in the end.

Murray Bodo
Cincinnati, Ohio
In the mirror year, 1991

---

[1] Eliot, T. S. "Little Gidding," *Four Quartets*. New York, N.Y.: Harcourt Brace Jovanovich, Inc., 1971, p. 59.

In Clare's Dormitory

I t has been three years now since I sat in your dormitory,
St. Clare, where I now sit in imagination. I hear again the
swallows screaming in the skies outside the open glassless
window that looks on Mount Subasio piling up and up from the
pink stones of Assisi's pueblo-like houses. It is oven-warm in
here, the stones of San Damiano glowing from the afternoon
sun's flames now flickering out in the west. It is quiet. The last
of the tourists' shoes are skittering at the end of the gravel path
where Marcello and Pepe and Nacisio stand and chat beside
their Fiats and Mercedes-Benz taxis.

I am alone with you, Clare, Chiara di Favarone, your
spirit lit with a fire apart from the sun. I touch the warm
stones, I kiss the spot where you laid your head those years,
bedridden, your needles hemming up the linen's fragile edges,
bordering the ragged ends.

I stand up and walk to the door from which the Blessed
Sacrament, the sun catching the gold of the ciborium, blinded
the Emperor Frederick's mercenary soldiers of their violent
purpose, and they retreated from your faith's awful power. I
slide open the wooden latch and open the door and look up
toward Assisi. I try to remember, to re-member the way it was
eight hundred years ago.

I try to see you writing your Rule of Life, writing
admonitions for your sisters, writing letters. My first image of

you is of a young girl fifteen or sixteen. Your hair, blond and in long heavy braids, is bound with bands of white linen that reach under your chin and around the crown of your head, leaving evenly-spaced gaps that reveal your golden braids. Your dress is of red velvet bordered at the neck with gold brocade that repeats in cloth the pattern of your braids. The sleeves are open on two sides to allow the puffed cotton undergarment to show. Every five or six inches buttons of gold-colored fabric secure a small braid that fastens the flaps of velvet sleeve, much like loose lacing on a boot fastens the two strips of leather across the tongue of a boot. Is there a dog at your side? And what is it you write with? A quill? And do you write on vellum?

Everything slows down in my imagining that scene. No swift pen or yellow pads of paper, no typewriter or word processor with reams of continuous paper like bolts of cloth feeding the printer. The very act of writing, quill to vellum, is slow, careful and (in your case, Clare) prayerful labor—like the needlework your fingers so painstaking plied for years, especially as you lay bedridden and ill at San Damiano those last years of your life.

And what were you wearing when you wrote the letters to Agnes of Prague? Sister Benvenuta says that you treated your body with such harshness that you were happy with one half-wool habit and one mantle. And if at any time you saw that the habit of a sister was poorer than the one you wore, you took off your own and gave the sister the better one.

And the last letters? Were you bedridden already? Sister Agnes said that you had a straw mat for a bed, and a bit of straw under your head; but after you were sick, on the order of Francis himself, you had a large sack of straw.

Are you sitting up in bed, and is there a breeze through the open window? And do you pause a lot as you write, or simply pen the words that flow spontaneously from within? Or am I asking the wrong questions, seeing in my mind's eye what is not necessary or helpful to your text? The written text of your letters perhaps. But not that text which is your life and which we know more about. Or do we? Or would that be looking into an outer mirror of who you were, instead of into that other mirror you wrote about to Agnes of Prague? Or is the velvet dress and the habit the image of the mirror you were looking into at that time—the outer mirroring the inner? I cannot answer these questions. I can only try to imagine the way it was with you....

A Springtime Story

I t is good in Assisi in the spring, when the poppies on the plain below the city break wild and red in the air. You walk beneath the clean blue heavens that spread the clouds above the mountains, and you are somewhere between two paradises—one overhead and one at your feet.

It is good in Assisi in the spring because this is the city where a love began, a love not diminished by the years. One man and one woman, Francis and Clare. So great was their love for God that even now, seven and a half centuries later, it makes Assisi good in spring and summer, fall and winter, too.

Their story, this Francis and this Clare, has been told many times; yet like every good story the telling of it is always new, and some further truth may be revealed in telling it again.

The Franciscan message is the story itself, and it has something to do with Assisi in the spring becoming summer, surrendering to the gentle mists of fall, lying seemingly dead in winter, and waiting for the poppies of another spring.

The lives of Francis and Clare are themselves seasons of every soul. This book is part of that story, Clare's story, and therefore Francis' story too. And it is more a story of springtime than any other season of the year. It is a story that looks heavenward but is always rooted in the poppy fields in the plain below Assisi.

Sky and earth and flowers.

The Treasure

S he followed him because she loved the treasure. She heard him speak of what he had found, and a passage in her own heart opened up. They had found the same treasure in different caves, and they would share it with whomever they met in that sacred place below the surface of life. She was Clare and he was Francis, and together they would show the world its hidden heart.

Clare was only eleven that day in the Piazza del Comune when she saw this young man gone "mad." He, the rich son of Pietro Bernardone, was making his way across the piazza, unkempt and haggard, begging food from the cursing citizens. Her young eyes were transfixed at this incredible sight, and she did not understand what he was doing. She, with her child's mind, thought he was funny and began to giggle, trying at the same time to wriggle free of her mother's firm grip. She wanted to run after him and join in all the mocking "fun" the grown-ups seemed to be having.

The following year when she was twelve, a strange scene was enacted between Francis and his father in the cathedral courtyard. Later she heard her parents talking in low voices about Francis, the wild twenty-four-year-old son of Bernardone, and of how he had renounced his father before Guido, the Bishop of Assisi. She wondered what "renounced" meant and why the bishop was there. But this time she didn't laugh. She sensed in her parents' voices a terrible seriousness. What Francis had done was something evil, something good children never do, and that night her sleep was filled with nightmares of beggars and bishops and fathers red with anger. Francis had already begun to haunt her.

By the time she was fourteen, he had become something of a celebrity, if still an oddity, a name on the lips of everyone in Assisi. He had repaired the crumbling churches of San Damiano, San Pietro and Our Lady of the Angels with stones he begged in the city. He lived with and nursed the lepers on the plain below Assisi, and he had changed his hermit's garb for that of a barefoot preacher.

And then she heard him preach. The words were simple and unadorned, but they touched her like a deep and purifying shaft of light. Her whole being seemed bathed in a light that came from somewhere inside her own heart.

What it was that Francis had opened up she did not know. It was not merely a fascination with Francis himself that drew her, but his words and something inside the words—the treasure—a secret, powerful force that came, she was sure, from God.

Her soul thirsted for more, and she longed to hear Francis whenever he preached to the people. But she was still in her teens and did not have the freedom to come and go as she pleased. She would, however, find a way. She would find a way because what was happening inside her came from God. She saw in Francis someone who must be experiencing what she felt in her own heart.

A New Love

She was in love! With God? With Francis? With both of them? With love? How did you sort it all out? Or should you? She was to learn over and over again the difference between loving and being in love, but this was the first time, and it was all too much for her.

She threw open the shutters of her bedroom and leaned out in the morning freshness, her gaze resting on the façade of the church of San Rufino, the patron saint of Assisi. She and Francis had been baptized in that church, and she had received her first Communion there. Her father's palazzo was adjacent to the church, so she had grown up, as it were, in the courtyard of the church of San Rufino. And now during this Lent of her eighteenth year, Francis had been preaching from its pulpit.

What he said inflamed her heart as nothing ever had before, but so did Francis himself. He seemed always to be looking only at her and to be speaking to her alone. At first this had disarmed her as she sat next to her parents in the first pew and looked into his penetrating brown eyes. How small he would look as he mounted the pulpit and how large he would grow with every word that struck her heart.

Did Francis know how she felt about him, did he wonder how he was going to handle what was happening inside the young, impressionable girl with the golden hair? Oh, how she missed him just thinking about him this Palm Sunday morning!

The sun had not yet climbed to the top of Mount Subasio, but the light of dawn had preceded it into the little square, and she kept her eyes on San Rufino. Shortly the town would begin to wake with the clatter of shutters, and bells would ring in the sun of another day. She would go to Palm Sunday services for the last time with her family.

For Francis and Bishop Guido had finally decided that this would be the day of her leaving the world to follow Jesus Christ as a spiritual daughter of Francis Bernardone. She would be the first woman to believe and follow the dream of poverty and littleness that God had given Francis for the rebuilding of God's kingdom.

And this very night it would all happen. Clare was so in love that the coming of night seemed an eternity away. These last hours would be the longest of her life, for just below the city in the little chapel of St. Mary of the Angels someone divine and someone human were waiting for her. She was in love, her heart rushing to begin loving.

A Consecrated Life

By her vows of poverty, chastity and obedience, Clare was wed forever to her Lord and Savior Jesus Christ; but in that solemn ceremony when Francis himself took her hair into his hands, cut through her curls and watched them fall onto the dirt floor of the chapel, something else happened as well: She was wed in mind and heart to Francis and the brothers.

Even externally she became like them. Clare put on a rough woolen habit. She secured it around the waist with an ordinary rope more beautiful to her than the jeweled belt she wore in her father's house. And with naked feet she stepped into a pair of wooden sandals that shone like golden slippers in the candlelight from Mary's tiny altar.

She would hold fast to the total poverty of this ecstatic moment till the end of her days. What greater union could there possibly be than union in the Lord? Clare viewed that moment of consecration in the Portiuncula[2] as a "sacrament" of her union with her Lord and with Francis and his brothers. They were now bound to her and she to them by their common consecration to the Lord. In some transcendent yet tangible way they were all building a new Eden in which men and women walked in the cool of the evening hand in hand with God.

The Lord stood between them, but he was transparent. Clare and the brothers saw themselves and everyone else even more clearly through the radiance of

---

[2]Portiuncula means "little portion" and is the term of endearment Francis used for the little chapel of Our Lady of the Angels.

Christ's glorified body. Jesus' presence made the union between human beings more real to Clare because it was a union beyond space and time and yet grounded in the most tangible of all realities, the human heart and mind, the human soul and body. Who could ask for more here where all is not yet perfect, here where evil is still a reality to be reckoned with, here where the cross is still the only chariot to heaven?

Those who observed Clare and Francis with purely human eyes would think they walked separately the road to God, that they were distinct and removed from one another. But if they had eyes of the spirit, they would see hearts inseparably joined, souls united in God. That was the mystery of spiritual love, and Clare wondered how many would have eyes to see it.

*After a few days, she moved to the
church of Sant' Angelo di Panzo.
But as her soul was not fully at rest there,
at the advice of the Blessed Francis she
removed at last to the church of San Damiano.*

Thomas of Celano

San Damiano

"A place for us." That is how she viewed the church of San Damiano. Once she was there, she and Agnes could live apart from Francis and the brothers and still be a part of the call to poverty and simplicity. Before coming to San Damiano she felt so alone. Francis and the brothers had one another, and wherever they were, they had a place to call home. The brotherhood *was* their home. She and Agnes needed something like that, too.

Immediately after Francis and the brothers had received her into the Order they took her to the Benedictine nuns of San Paolo near Bastia. A few days later she moved to another Benedictine convent, Sant' Angelo di Panzo on the slopes of Mount Subasio. There she was joined by her sister Agnes, a girl of fifteen, who like Clare had run away from her home to give her life to God.

But Clare and Agnes were not Benedictines, and they felt alone and removed from the brothers. So Clare asked Francis for a home where she and Agnes could live the new way of life he had given them. And Francis

11

understood and blessed their request.

He begged the church of San Damiano from the Bishop of Assisi and gave it to Clare and Agnes so they would have a place on this earth where they could live the perfect poverty of Jesus Christ. Soon Clare and Agnes were joined by Pacifica, Benvenuta, Cecilia and Philippa. Clare was at peace, for now there was a sisterhood that was a home.

San Damiano was the small chapel where Francis had heard the voice of Christ from the crucifix, "Francis, go and repair my house which, as you see, is entirely in ruins." Francis had done as the Lord commanded. He restored this little church, prophesying as he did so that some day this would be the home of the Poor Ladies of the Lord.

How this fact filled Clare with joy! The home Francis had given the Poor Ladies was the very place where his own call from God had begun. How well he had understood their request. This church was so much a part of him. Here he had worked in the sweat of his brow, begging stones in Assisi and mortaring them into place. Here in his fear he had hidden from his father's wrath, and here he had learned in prayer how to overcome fear and face his father.

In choosing this particular place he had given the Poor Ladies the place where he had learned to listen to the Lord, the place where the crucified Jesus became a mirror of Francis' own soul. Yes, Francis had understood what they were asking. It was truly a place for them, a mirror of what Clare longed for all of them to become.

Her union with him was so complete and harmonious, her mind and heart so like his own, that it is difficult to know how much was conscious imitation on her part and how much natural endowment.

Lothar Hardick, O.F.M.

Pilgrims in Spirit

She had known almost at once that she would follow him. The first time she heard Francis preach, his words pierced her heart with love for Jesus, and Francis' soul was one with hers. She soon learned, however, that they could never be together, for then they would not be free, they would not be who they really were, two pilgrims in love with the Lord, two souls who were closer apart than they could ever be together. Together they might end up loving each other more than the treasure they had found in one another's heart.

She had heard the echo of her own voice in Francis' words, and he had found in her the incarnation of every word he spoke. They were pilgrims in spirit, poor and wandering hearts in love with God; and knowing they loved each other in the same God and shared that love with their brothers and sisters, they were never lonely.

Clare drew her ideals from Francis' words, and Francis, she felt, drew his words at times from the inspiration of her life. She made it possible for him to believe that what he spoke was livable, that the gospel life brought joy indeed, that every word Jesus uttered could be lived by those who heard his words with open hearts.

Clare hoped that she and the Poor Ladies would become the living proof of everything Francis believed in. Was that why she'd had to follow him the moment she heard him speak? Had they been fashioned for each other out of the longing of the ages? Had they known each other longer than they knew?

*Because by divine inspiration you've made
yourselves daughters and servants of the most high
King, the heavenly Father, and have taken the
Holy Spirit as spouse, choosing to live according
to the perfection of the Holy Gospel, I am resolved
and promise for myself and for my brothers to
have the same loving care and special solicitude for
you as I have for them.*

Form of Life given by St. Francis
to St. Clare and her sisters
(1212-1213)

Sister and Brother Planets

T hough he had brought her to the Lord, Francis
was not always on her mind. In fact, Clare
dwelled so much in God that Francis was seldom
in her thoughts. At the same time he was always in her
thoughts. How this could be, she did not fully understand.
She only knew that her real lover and beloved was the
Lord and that Francis was intimately related to her love
for Jesus. Her preoccupation was not with Francis, but
with her Lord. She loved Francis but was not dependent
upon him as she had been at first.

How hard it had been in the beginning. The first
time Clare understood that she and Francis could never
be together she wept. She was only eighteen at the time,
and at that blessed time of youth so many things seem
unfair which later prove to have been providential. But
"then" was not "later"; it was the full flowering of her

adolescence. This made everything vague and unclear in her mind like the perpetual haze that lay over the valley of Spoleto. She only knew that she would love him forever and that their marriage of mind and heart was already a fact. Why she loved a man twelve years older than she when so many young men her own age sought her love, she never even considered; for she never thought of Francis' age. She just loved him in whom she saw the face of Jesus. She was in love with Francis' soul.

She understood now that they each had a mission to fulfill, that they moved in separate but concentric spheres that centered on the Lord. Their intimacy was not with each other but with God. Yet Clare never doubted that her closeness to the Lord effected a growing closeness to Francis. She understood, as Francis did, that preoccupation with each other would destroy the center and separate them from God and from each other, broken circles shooting crazily off into space.

But the center *would* hold, for they both uncompromisingly looked upon the Lord, she in prayer and contemplation at San Damiano and Francis everywhere upon the road. His orbit was wider than hers, reaching out to the length and breadth of Italy and beyond, even to England and the Holy Land. Hers lay inside of his, drawing Francis to the center and holding her tightly between Francis and God. They were like sister and brother planets encircling the Lord.

Roses

She loved flowers on the altar. Roses especially reminded her of who she was and of what she must become. They were so tight at first, and then slowly, imperceptibly they opened up and surrendered themselves to whatever lay about them. Even in dying they dropped their petals gracefully; and if you listened quietly enough, you could hear the silence of their falling. All that was left was the center, naked and free of all the pampering satin petals it held so closely at the start. And the center held in perfect poverty.

Jesus

Jesus, always Jesus smoldering in her heart, then flaming up suddenly, surprising her with the ardor of his love. No matter how intensely she looked to Francis for teaching and guidance, for friendship and brotherhood, he never replaced Jesus as Lord and master of her heart and soul. And Jesus proved over and over again his love for her. Always, even when she was beginning to despair of his love, he would return suddenly, unexpectedly, the warmth of his entry as soft as the morning sun upon the white roses of her little garden. Her Lord always knew when his seeming distance was causing havoc in her heart. She would turn inward and pray aloud in her anguish, begging Jesus to come to her and fill the void. And the Lord would remain silent and away.

Then, when she was not praying but working in her garden, or nursing her sick sisters, or working at her sewing, it would happen—with a sudden rush of warmth he would be there, saving her again, rewarding her patience with his presence and the power of his healing. And he would seem to come from within as if he had in fact been smoldering in her heart with just enough spark to be re-enkindled by the Spirit—that Spirit like the wind, blowing where he would and refusing to be harnessed by any magic formula of prayer.

Slowly she learned to wait upon the Lord and his Spirit, to open her mind and heart like thirsty ground waiting for rain, like rose petals waiting for the sun. And if she waited in patience and continued to work faithfully at whatever was at hand, the Lord would always surprise her, sometimes meeting her in the kitchen, sometimes in the laundry, sometimes in the refectory, sometimes even when she was sweeping the earthen floor with nothing particular on her mind.

Waiting

From trying to pray well, Clare learned a lot about loving God. For one thing she learned that love involves waiting. You waited for your beloved to come upon the mountaintops; you waited for just a glimpse of him bounding across the valley of your loneliness, and like a gazelle he was restless and seldom stayed long with you. And if you were too dependent on his visits, his tangible presence, then most of the time you felt lonely and frustrated, and your thoughts were preoccupied with the beloved and his next coming. And so you learned to live as independently of his felt presence as possible. You learned to expect little and to greet every visitation as a gift, a surprise that would happen when you least expected it.

You prayed for his coming, but you were wise not to let your longing, your loneliness interfere with living, with what had to be done from moment to moment. You kept giving even when you felt nothing in return. And most of all, you learned to trust your beloved, to know deep within that love did not depend on your experience of his presence. In fact, most of the time his love was a felt absence that prepared the heart for the ecstasy of meeting once again.

Life with Jesus was a drama of finding and losing, of separation and reunion. The price you paid for ecstatic union was the loneliness and heartache of continued separation, of wondering if he had abandoned you, had ceased loving you. With the Lord, Clare experienced at times the ecstatic union of mind and heart and soul and body; the intervals between his visitations caused her more pain than she cared to think about. She tried not to remember the intervals; they would, after all, continue to recur without her dwelling on them. She tried to live in the present, hoping and praying, but not depending too much on the coming of her beloved. And by living in the present Clare gradually learned that the contemplative life is not a living for ecstasy but a simple faith that knows the Lord is always present whether or not his presence is felt in any tangible way.

Clare was a vessel of humility, a shrine of
chastity, a flame of love, the essence of kindness,
the strength of patience, the bond of peace, and
the source of loving unity in her community: meek
in word, gentle in deed, lovable and beloved in all
things.... In the lifetime of Clare the power of her
holiness shone forth in many different miracles.
Thus she restored to one of the Sisters of her
monastery the use of her voice,...to another,...
she restored the power to speak correctly,...for
another she opened her deaf ear so that she could
hear. By making the sign of the cross over them,
she freed others from fever...and other maladies.

Document of Canonization

Love

D oes the love of God mean the end of human love
for those who embrace the virginal life? Clare
hoped her love for Francis, for his brothers and
for the Poor Ladies of San Damiano, proved to everyone
that her vow of chastity had made her warm and gentle
and full of love for everyone whose life she touched.

Human love was for her the only way to divine love,
for what in fact is the love of God if not love of the Body
of Christ? God had become human, and it was in this
Body of his that he was to be found and loved. It was the
human body which was the instrument of loving. One
who withdrew from another was somehow frightened of
people, deluded into believing that God was only spirit.

21

God had indeed become human, flesh was now inspirited, and Clare treated people accordingly.

Francis realized the great faith she had in Christ's presence in his Mystical Body. He was always sending people to her, and she would lay her hands on them and ask the Lord to heal them.

How fitting, somehow, how like Francis to know that San Damiano, dedicated to the Roman physicians, Saints Cosmas and Damian, must continue to be a place of healing. The spirit of this place was a healing spirit. And that healing would continue in Clare.

Cicadas

She heard his name every day in the olive trees, the cypresses and the low bushes surrounding San Damiano. "Dio, Dio, Dio!" That is what the chorus of cicadas seemed to be singing. They reminded her of her Lord because she believed God was singing through them as God sang through all of creation. God's song was in everything because she heard with ears of faith and because she strove to love God without reservation of any kind.

To love the Lord with her whole heart and her whole mind and her whole soul! That is what Clare wanted above all else in life. Everything, including Francis and his new way of life, was secondary to her all-consuming desire to love the Lord, her God. God was in her mind and in her heart, in her speech and in her silence, in her work and in her rest, in her waking and in her sleeping, in her eyes and ears and mouth and nose and fingertips.

"Dio, Dio, Dio! God, God, God!" God was the secret of what she and her Poor Ladies were all about. And the cicadas kept reminding all of them that God was a song in the ears of the believer, a melody in the heart.

She was the new woman of the Valley of Spoleto, who poured forth a new fountain of the water of life....

Document of Canonization

A New Jerusalem

Though Clare loved the Lord with her whole heart, Francis was also a part of that love. Sorting that out was not difficult because the two had always been associated in her mind. She did not love God in the abstract but rather as she saw God incarnate in Francis. She had found the God she heard in her heart speaking in Francis. Wherever one was, there was the other also. And she never thought this feeling divided her love.

Over the years Clare grew in the conviction that God was present to her in every person she met, and it all began with Francis in their Eden of Assisi. That is why she loved Assisi so. Their love began there, the three of them: Francis, Clare and the Lord; Creation, Clare and the Creator.

As a young girl, before she was finally cloistered at San Damiano, Clare with her mother, Ortolana, used to walk the streets of Assisi, making every corner of the city her own. There were eleven gates to the city, and after she met Francis, she always viewed them as the gates of a New Jerusalem. She and Francis had been graced with the care of this new city that had descended from on high. Out of Assisi's gates would flow the living waters of Christ, and into Assisi would stream the chosen people of this new city. They would come to Assisi seeking the Lord who had been revealed anew in his servant Francis.

Clare believed that Assisi was a sacred city and that she and her Poor Ladies had been given a position on God's holy mountain second only to Francis himself. Somehow she sensed also that her name would be forever linked with that of Francis. They were "married" forever as the Adam and Eve of a new family in the Church of God.

The Lord had built for them a new Jerusalem called Assisi, and men and women from every corner of the earth would come there hoping that this new Eden was not just a dream, a fantasy spread by the idle tongues of travelers. And she knew they would not be disappointed. The lovers among them would understand why two shared her heart, why God chose a man *and* a woman to build his New Jerusalem, and why a pure and virginal love begets so many children in the Lord.

When she was yet a maiden in the world,
she sought from a tender age to pass through
this...world by the path of the pure and to
guard the precious treasure of her virginity in
unstained modesty.... Noble by birth, but
more noble by her manner of life, she preserved
above all under this holy Rule the virginity
which she previously guarded so well.

   Document of Canonization

Chastity

Somehow she was sure she was an important part of Francis' chastity. In loving her as he did, Francis turned his love toward a woman as chaste as he was, a woman who reminded him of his Lady Poverty and the Blessed Virgin. Clare felt humble in thinking that; nor was that thought really pride, because it was true, and truth has nothing of pride in it.

She liked to think that when Francis was tempted, he would turn his thoughts to her and see in her the Lady Poverty, who dwelled apart from him, inaccessible in her vowed love, like the ideal woman whom a man imagines will purify his love, and somehow does.

She remembered Brother Angelo telling her of that night in the tower in Rome when Francis cried out that he was afraid to be alone, and Brother Angelo stayed with him. Clare hoped she was there, too, in his thoughts, her presence a shield against insomnia and fear. Francis would never be alone as long as she loved him, for her love reached out from San Damiano, an embrace of spirit forever extended toward Francis and his brothers.

Words

Words! How important they had been to her from the first time she heard Francis preach, and especially from that Lent of her eighteenth year when Francis inspired her to leave her home and join him and his brothers at the Portiuncula. She had hung upon his every word as if his words were life itself.

Later she would listen to Francis preach and speak, and his words became God's words for her and her Ladies at San Damiano. And over the years, when he was troubled or in doubt, Francis would send to Clare for her words. Her words were not only balm to his spirit, but he immediately acted upon them as spirit and life from the Lord.

In a way she did not fully understand, the Lord Jesus became tangible in their midst whenever they spoke together. They met, bringing from separate caves the Christ each had found in solitude, and the Word became flesh in their sharing him. He became the Lord of their union, and he was the same Christ each had found in the silence of prayer and penance.

Each was so intimately united in mind and heart with Christ that their union with each other was made perfect in him. At least, this is how Clare saw it, and she praised the Lord for the wonder of his gift to her through Francis.

She almost said to her *and* Francis, but that would not be true. From the very beginning the Lord had called her *through* Francis. He was the Lord's instrument, the voice God had used to call her out of her father's house into the new and wonderful world of the Spirit.

And by using Clare as his voice, God in his providence let her repay Francis. Once, for example, when Francis was worried about his future, wondering whether he should retire from the life of apostolic preaching and devote himself entirely to prayer and contemplation, he sent Brother Masseo to Clare for her advice and counsel. She immediately went to one of her sisters, and they prayed together for God's answer. And while they prayed, both women heard deep in their hearts the same words: "I have not called Francis for his own sake alone, but that he may reap a harvest of souls and that many may be saved through him."

Brother Masseo later told Clare that her words were identical to those of Brother Sylvester, whom Francis had also consulted. Francis had received these words with great joy and immediately set out to preach to the people of God. Clare's own heart was filled with peace and joy at this news because she had become for Francis what he was for her, the word of the Lord!

Days of Heartache

T hen came the days of heartache and pain when she felt Francis slowly moving away from her and the other Poor Ladies of San Damiano. At first he had come to see them and to preach to them the Good News of Jesus. Then, without explanation, his visits grew less and less frequent and finally stopped altogether.

Clare supposed it had something to do with fidelity and Francis' deep inner need to be one and undivided. But she could not understand how she and the Poor Ladies could bring division to his heart, for their own fidelity to Christ and Francis' vision had been tested and found true and unswerving.

Perhaps Francis saw things differently. He was everything she and the Poor Ladies loved and dreamed of becoming; he brought them happiness and joy. He led them constantly to Jesus and made their love for the Lord alive and glowing in the Spirit. Were they something different to him? Did they come between him and the Lord he loved so much?

If that were true, how ironic it would be, for Lady Poverty's daughters would then be mere distractions for the man who had brought them to God. How could a love like theirs cause Francis such anxiety and make him so unsure of himself? Perhaps that was it; their love was pure and good and therefore like a magnet for Francis. It drew him to the castle of San Damiano instead of to his Lord.

But that made no sense at all to Clare, for people did just the opposite in her life: They led her closer and closer to the God who had become incarnate in them. But then she realized what she and Francis did share, their deep fidelity to the Lord, and she knew this one difference between them was the price she would have to pay for being part of God's plan for Francis. And having said that to herself, she still didn't like it—and never would.

Contemplation

C lare sat quietly in her little garden and surrendered her senses to everything around her. It was like opening up to God, and this, she knew, was a part of contemplation. If you closed yourself up and feared your senses, then contemplation was impossible. She loved to sit in her garden and experience the fullness of creation through sight and sound and touch and smell, and even the taste of the breeze scented with ginestra and oleander, rosemary and myrtle.

Often she would rise at four in the morning and go out to her garden just to listen to the dawn. *Listen* was the right word because dawn meant the whole sky would be alive with swallows screaming crazily in the morning light. Swallows *were* morning in Assisi.

Sometimes, too, she would sit in the late afternoon and look up at Mount Subasio and remember how, as a child, she used to pretend to steal away to her cliff on the mountain. From there she would imagine looking back at the Rocca Maggiore with the ends of the city walls clinging to it as arms to a strong body. She loved her imaginary cliff, for there she could be alone and touch the earth, whisper back to the trees and inhale the spirit of the mountain.

And then there was Francis. No matter where he was, she could see him and hear him. She could feel again the touch of his eyes on hers when she visited him as a young girl. She could still smell his frail body through the strong scent of sweat trapped in the wool of his habit.

His taste was that of the wilderness. As a young girl she used to pull out blades of grass or weeds and put them to her mouth, and whenever she saw Francis or talked to him that wild taste of plants and leaves and twigs filled her imagination. He was a man who lived in the woods and slept in caves; he always had soil and grass clinging to his robe. She imagined his taste was more plant than animal.

Or maybe it was his gentleness and quiet that brought plants into her mind. There was nothing of animal fierceness in Francis. There was only courtesy and kindness and a delicate, gentle yet strong nature that reminded her of trees. Maybe that was why she used to hug trees when she was young and deeply in love with Francis. People would surely have thought her crazy, but her first love for Francis was as young as she was at the time. Whenever she was lonely or did not understand his distance and reserve, she would embrace a tree and feel comforted in some strange, inexplicable way.

All these memories and more were hidden away in her garden. Small as it was, it contained so much of what she needed for contemplation and intimacy, union with God and people and nature.

Camelot

To love what Francis loved you had to love knighthood and chivalry. Though he had turned his back on war, he never ceased to be a courteous knight at heart. Everything he did spoke of chivalry and the knightly code, and to understand that was to understand in large part the marvelous man whose very name reminded Clare of the troubadours.

As a girl, she, like Francis, had listened to the troubadours from Provence and northern Italy. She too had been captivated by their songs and the stories of Arthur and his knights. In some mysterious way she and the Poor Ladies and Francis and the brothers were a part of that story of King Arthur. Out of those childhood memories transformed now by the love of God, they walked into the real world, ladies of the castle and knights upon the road.

No longer the fantasy of youth, there was still, despite its earnestness, an element of play in this little drama that they were enacting for all the world to see. It was a tale of chivalry they were living, a new tale with Christ himself as the king and liege lord. There was also a new dimension of joy which Francis brought to the old chivalric ideals of total devotion to the lord, courtesy toward everyone and selfless compassion for the poor and weak.

The love of their lives was unintelligible apart from Camelot, for that world of the Round Table explained the nobility of the brothers and Poor Ladies and made them different from other beggars of their time. Like the poor they lived in utter poverty, but their faces shone. Their bearing was such that everyone who met them saw who they really were beneath their peasant garbs; their hands outstretched to beg somehow invited others to kneel and kiss a hidden royalty.

Clare loved this element of chivalry. For far from lowering her self-esteem, the poverty the Poor Ladies shared made her feel like a true Lady in God's castle. This poverty was not penance or self-flagellation or gloomy asceticism. It was putting on the Lord Jesus Christ, who had emptied himself taking the form of a servant. And who, wearing the garments of the great King himself, could denigrate self, or be ashamed?

In this new world of godly knights and ladies, beggars could walk with pride and self-esteem, for they were heralds of the great King. And those who announced the good news of God's coming did not walk around depressed, beating their breasts. They put on rags and raised their heads. And everyone with eyes to see rejoiced that the countryside was once again peopled by lords and ladies whose court was a movable Camelot open to simple folk from every land, a Camelot where every man and woman could put on the royal robes of Lady Poverty and walk again with pride.

Swords in the Sunlight

T he Kingdom! Always the Kingdom and its upbuilding! The discipline of her life, her penance, her poverty—these were heroic ideals because she would be a lady, a spouse of Christ the King. She and the Poor Ladies of San Damiano would do at home the great deeds Francis and the brothers did upon the road. Nor would they be outdone, for they were noble and fine, ladies fit for great knights like the brothers. Together they would shine that the Lord Jesus might be glorified.

Clare, from the beginning, recognized the heroic in everything she and Francis did. They grew into adulthood, but they never left that part of adolescence which kept them ever faithful to their ideal. What they did was hard, but it was a hardness that shone, a hardness that polished the soul.

It polished the soul because it was all for the love of Jesus and the building of the kingdom, and the cost was never too high. It was all for Christ who had been crucified for them. Clare knew that the life of a lady in this new kingdom was the daily carrying of the cross, but it was a task that was noble and fine because the wood of her cross was cut from the cross of Jesus, her Lord and King. And if you carried that cross, your life gradually acquired a new dignity. You experienced a new freedom and your step began to lighten.

Clare noticed, too, that the cross slowed you down so you could see more along the way. You couldn't hurry when you were carrying a cross. You began to notice the stones beneath your feet. You saw pain in the eyes of those you passed and how important it was to them that you bear your cross like a true lady. They were encouraged seeing your cheerfulness and the light in your eyes; and they also looked up the road to see where you were going with such grand determination. You were building the kingdom all along the way, and if you dared look back, you would see a multitude following you, their crosses gleaming like swords in the sunlight.

A Kingdom of the Heart

Jesus. How much that name meant to her! It summoned up everything she wanted in life. So many people in Assisi were busy and anxious, acquiring and building up little perishable kingdoms that consumed much of their energy. And still they were unhappy. But with the simple sound of Jesus' name in her heart Clare could summon up her own kingdom, a kingdom of the heart where her Lord dwelt and where he would reign forever.

It was difficult for Clare to understand how anyone could really abandon this inner kingdom for superficialities and transient pursuits. But she realized, too, that Jesus was a gift. Not everyone had enjoyed her privileged background, or her friendship with a prophet of the Lord like Francis.

But did they not know their own emptiness and seek to fill it with something more than ceaseless talk and busyness and the inflation of their own selves? Surely they did. And that is why she repeated Jesus' name over and over again. She was asking him to send Francis' brothers to the ends of the earth with the message that Jesus fills, Jesus satisfies, Jesus answers those questions people are afraid to ask.

Clare saw herself and all her Poor Ladies as the virgins of a new temple that would draw the whole world to Assisi as to a new oracle. There God had spoken a unique message reaffirming the incarnation of God's Son and setting a new sun in the sky in the person of Francis. The dawn that was Francis would be a turning point in human movement toward wholeness and union with God.

On what future mountaintop would mind and heart unite to draw people finally and inevitably to their destiny? And what new prophet would complete what Francis was here continuing? Jesus! Would it not be Jesus returning who would stand on the last mountaintop, drawing all the earth to himself? Where that would be didn't matter, really. It would be wherever Jesus set his foot. And all the gods of every time and place would dwell in a temple inhabited by a triune God, for all the divine creations of every civilization were partial revelations snatched from God's whispers to those who tried to hear him. In the end his full voice would stand embodied upon the final pinnacle of space and time. That is what Clare prayed for every time she summoned up in mind and voice the Alpha and Omega, Jesus Christ!

*There were times when he was afraid he
was too reserved in his attitude toward her and
that he stood at too great a distance from her.
But she never disappeared completely from
his thoughts. She was the perfect fulfillment
of his dream and his holy task.*

Auspicius van Corstanje, O.F.M.

To Love From Afar

Clare eventually understood the distance at which
Francis kept her and why. Very simply, he did,
after all, believe she threatened his all-
consuming love for God. She didn't, of course; but
Francis thought she might: He was afraid, perhaps, not of
her, but of himself. She had seen that in others; they
seemed to be afraid of someone or something when it was
only themselves they feared. Clare knew, in fact, that no
one understood the singleness of Francis' love for Jesus
better than she did. And no one would more faithfully
protect that love than she.

But because Francis was the kind of man he was, he
could never allow anyone, even Clare, to rest even in the
corner of his eye. His eyes were fixed entirely on the Lord.
If he saw you in looking on the Lord, that was wonderful.
But if he saw you between him and God or was distracted
by glimpsing you out of the corner of his eye, then he
would run away and beg the Lord's forgiveness for his
"unfaithfulness."

Sometimes, though he was older, she felt like

scolding him for being so childish. But then she would remember that he *was* a child—and scolding might make him grow up. It was, after all, the child in him that made him so lovable, so different from the grim, so-called saints she had heard about in childhood stories.

But what was she going to do with such an impossible man with such a single-hearted love of God? What could she do, after all, except love God and let Francis be free? She would love him from afar, and she would thereby be near in a way that did not frighten him.

The Power of Prayer

How she had struggled with her heart during those months after she heard Francis preach in San Rufino's and San Giorgio's. It was difficult to explain, even years later, the mesmerizing effect he had on her. And what made it even more difficult for her, she knew then as she knew now, was that Francis was praying for her.

That is what made his preaching so different from others'. He not only preached the word of God, but he took the responsibility for his words and became involved with the people to whom he preached. One way he did this was to pray incessantly that the word God spoke through him would penetrate the souls of his hearers and change their lives.

And so Clare had been swept away both by Francis'

preaching and by the intercessory power of his prayer. She felt helpless and dizzy inside as wave after wave of God's grace washed over her. Every time she tried to stand up a new wave would hit her, and she could feel herself weakening in her struggle with God.

All along Clare knew that if she would only surrender, she would float easily in the immensity of God's love. But floating meant letting go of too many things she loved and clung to for her to surrender easily. There was her family first of all, the love and tenderness of her parents and the affection and closeness she felt for her sisters. Other things, too, were good and beautiful to her. Her young heart found it difficult to understand why anyone should have to turn loose of them to follow a Christ who himself proclaimed the goodness of creation and the love of God for everything which God had made, even for the nervous little sparrows who clung so close to the earth though they could fly.

But Francis continued to pray, and in the end he and his God won. Together they were too much for her, a lesson she never forgot in all the ensuing years when she prayed for others. When you prayed, you were never alone. It was you and God together entering into the very depths of the person for whom you prayed. And though the person might at first sense your entry as an invasion, ultimately it was your forceful entry that broke down the doors of fear and hatred imprisoning the heart.

Over and over again surrender brought freedom and release of pent-up frustrations and longings for love. There in the core of the other, you and God would take up residence, and the person would experience true love for the first time. And another person of prayer would begin to join with God in assaulting the yet unvanquished hearts of countless ailing members of Christ's Body.

All of this and more she learned while struggling with herself and God and other people. And like any person in love she never forgot her first lessons in love, her first knowledge of the ways of her beloved.

They discovered in each other the same
luxury of God's presence and the same fire
that consumed all the idols in their hearts,
until they were ash.

Auspicius van Corstanje, O.F.M.

A Vacancy for God

"For the love of my Lord and Savior Jesus Christ!" How often and with what fervor Francis repeated that phrase! Clare understood much of Francis from his love of chivalry, but his love for Jesus crucified opened up his real being. He was a man in love with his Lord. No person or thing would ever detract from his love, from his single-hearted devotion to Christ.

Clare understood that, for she, too, was in love with the Lord. That they had in common, and that love of God would never change.

But sometimes she wondered what it would be like if the brothers and Poor Ladies could work more closely together for the Lord. What was it that separated men and women in the kingdom? Why did they have to work apart rather than together? Or did they really work together though apart?

She only knew that she would never abandon Francis and the brothers. No matter how far they roamed or how long they stayed away, Clare and the Poor Ladies would always faithfully love them. She would never abandon the Lord's knights as the Lord never abandoned her. That was what she knew of love: The Lord was faithful and would not leave his people. And Clare, participating in his love, would remain faithful to her loves as well, for that was what she knew of love.

She saw Francis' fidelity in everything he did and in his constant refrain, "for the love of my Lord and Savior Jesus Christ." No matter how engaged Francis was with any other activity or how ardently he worked with or loved the people of God, he always left room at the center of his heart for God. He left a vacancy for God that only God could occupy. There in that open space in her own heart she also met God. She, too, always left a vacancy for God. But when the Lord came to dwell there, he brought Francis with him, and Clare's spirit joined with Francis in praising God.

The love of their Lord and Savior Jesus Christ secured that vacancy in the center of the Poor Ladies' and the brothers' hearts and made possible their love for one another. God is love and those who love God remain somehow in one another. Clare and Francis and those who followed in their footsteps would remain united forever, for the center of their love was the eternal God.

A Faithful God

Clare noticed as she grew older that she was slowly becoming what she had always dreamed of being; she was slowly realizing the potential within her through the action of God. Everything that had happened to her through the years she now saw as a part of God's plan for her.

It was a matter of trust and believing at first. Once you had persevered, it was a matter of seeing that what you hoped could happen, was in fact happening all along. You grew into that fullness which is Christ, and you knew that God was indeed faithful to his word.

Such growth comes to those who believe an inner voice, those with hope for the future, those who love when all is still a promise unfulfilled. Faith, after all, is where it all begins. In faith you believe that God loves you, and you are made good by God's creative loving. And only the one who first believed in you really makes it possible for you to believe in yourself. You live and love in the stormy, unrealized present, clinging to the glimpse of the future given by hope. Eventually, the dream you believed, the future you hoped in becomes the present, and suddenly you see clearly that it is all realized from moment to moment. When you are aware of the future, open to its presence, the presence *is* the future.

God was accomplishing something new in the world through the brothers and the Poor Ladies, something they had dared to believe in when it still wore the vague colors of a dream.

Rainy Days

There were days when the rains would come and settle in over the whole valley of Spoleto. But rain never depressed her. On the contrary, it was a source of encouragement, because Clare knew that somewhere out there on the side of Mount Subasio Francis and the brothers were burrowing into their small caves where they would rediscover the love of God in themselves and pray intently over it until the skies cleared. They would emerge renewed and ready to share the newly found treasure with others.

True, she worried especially about the physical pain and suffering Francis endured in all those damp caves, but she knew he would never change the pattern of penance in his life. So identified was he with the poor suffering Christ that he considered every pain and deprivation a privilege, an opportunity to share in the sufferings of his Lord.

Clare understood that kind of love because it was in her as well. She, however, suffered not only with her Lord, but with Francis, and she knew in some strange, intuitive way when Francis was suffering. Rain was only one reminder among many. She knew and loved Francis so well that there was an invisible bond of communication between them that was continually carrying felt messages to and fro. Love was that real to Clare, and what she heard and understood in prayer was not that different an experience from what she heard and understood intuitively from Francis. Love made both experiences possible, and it explained why the language of lovers and mystics was the same. She thought that rain, too, might be something she had in common with other lovers.

Choosing God's Will

You choose your vocation over and over again. It is not a decision made once for all time when one is young. Clare chose her life at San Damiano again and again, and each time she embraced the life of poverty she did so for slightly different reasons. As she grew in experience and understanding of her commitment, she had to say yes again and again to a way of life that was not exactly the life she expected at the beginning.

She never knew, for example, how hard it would be to give up the love and companionship of her family until those dark days and nights when God seemed to have abandoned her and the original enthusiasm of serving the Lord died out. She knew then that the honeymoon of her relationship with God was over and that she had to rededicate herself to her heavenly spouse, a spouse different from the one she had originally imagined.

Her life with Francis, too, turned out different from what she had thought it would be. In the enthusiasm of her eighteenth year she had thought they would be together in the service of the Lord, that she and other Poor Ladies would go about the countryside with Francis and his brothers, caring for them and supporting them like the women in the Gospel who accompanied Jesus on the road and who were so much a part of his life on earth. How different that all turned out to be! She saw less of the brothers than anyone and she remained in the monastery of San Damiano all her life.

What an adjustment that **was**! She had to recommit herself to a presence in the world totally other than the one she had once dreamed of. Her presence to Francis and his brothers was only in prayer; her journey involved no road but that which leads into the heart. She who had bargained for the contemplative *and* apostolic life and who longed to travel to Morocco as a missionary remained a cloistered contemplative;[3] but in embracing her life as God slowly revealed it to her, she ended up an apostle in a way she never envisioned for herself and her Poor Ladies.

God himself chose the manner of your witness. In embracing God's will, you discovered a self you did not know you could be, you discovered a part of yourself you would never have known in pursuing your own will alone.

To be open and sensitive to God's will! How difficult that was, because it meant accepting change and re-embracing your emerging self. You always wanted to stop at some lower level because no matter how difficult the ascent, once you arrived there, you could relax and be comfortable. But then God would call again, and if you wanted to grow, you would have to let go of your comfort and risk a further climb.

---

[3]Clare and her sisters lived a cloistered life (certainly from 1219 on) since the rule prescribed this in strict terms. However, the sources of her life tell us that they did not always abide by it, thus revealing the existence of another way of living at San Damiano....

"Celano as well as the sisters of San Damiano note in the process of canonization certain liberties regarding the cloister: it was open to persons who did not share the life of the monastery, to the Friars Minor: to the brothers who begged (C. 61), to Brother Stephen who was cured by Clare and who slept in the monastery (C. 32), and Clare herself on her deathbed 'desired the presence of priests and holy brothers' (C. 45). Brother Juniper went to San Damiano. Sometimes the account of cures teaches us that certain sick people were in the cloister (C. 33, Process IV and IX, 6). There is also an account of a meeting betweeen Clare and Francis at the Portiuncula....

"The details related above as well as certain accounts and witnesses prove her great freedom compared to the orientation adopted by Hugolin in behalf of the first Poor Clares. They also highlight her personal conception regarding the imitation of Christ and her faithfulness to this conception." Heribert Roggen, *The Spirit of St. Clare* (Chicago, Ill.: Franciscan Herald Press, 1971), pp. 76-79.

When Summer Comes
and the Roses Are in Bloom

A story was told in Assisi which, though it was not true, did capture something of what she and Francis suffered. Clare loved the story from the very first time she heard it because it was filled with sympathy and understanding and because it contained one of those delightful little miracles that were so much a part of the lives of the saints which she had heard as a young girl.

It seems that one winter's day she and Francis were on the road from Spello to Assisi. (Already a folk legend was surrounding them, for they had never walked that road together!) It was a walk people said the Lady Clare dearly loved because it wound through the valley of Spoleto. Even now as it lay covered with fresh snow, it was more beautiful than any landscape she knew. She and Francis were both depressed and the cold seemed to cut through their rough clothes more bitterly than when they had left Assisi earlier that day.

Clare suspected that they were both thinking the same thing, that their low spirits resulted from what had happened along the way. They had knocked on several doors to beg for bread and water; and though the kind peasants had generously given them food, Clare and Francis noticed the suspicion and disapproval in their eyes. They had also heard several unpleasant insinuations which, even though full of laughter and good cheer, had hurt them. They walked in silence, night falling quickly around them.

Suddenly Francis broke the silence: "Lady, you heard what the people are saying about us." A great lump lay in her throat and she could not answer. She was afraid that if she tried, she would start crying. They walked in tense silence. Finally, Francis said haltingly, "We have to walk apart, Clare. You can be back at San Damiano before it is dark. I'll follow you at a distance, so you won't be afraid."

His words were too much for her and she sank to her knees in the road. She knelt with her face in her hands and then suddenly stood up and started down the road with her head bowed. She forced herself not to look back.

The road turned into the forest and Clare could feel the rapid beating of her heart as she neared the forest's edge. She felt she was leaving him forever and she could not face that kind of future without some word of comfort and hope. She stopped and turned and cried out in a broken voice, "Francis, when will we see each other again?" Francis answered gently, "When summer comes and the roses are in bloom."

Then Clare stood open-mouthed and trembling. For from the snow-covered tops of bushes and small trees, roses began to appear in full bloom. Clare opened her arms and walked hesitantly to a small bush. She picked the roses tenderly, filling the folds of her habit with blossoms. She turned and walked back to Francis and let the roses fall through his open hands onto the clean white snow. From that day on they were never really separated again, though they saw each other seldom. Though the years came and went, the roses in her garden bloomed every summer for her and her Francis.[4]

---

[4]This legend is found in *Francis of Assisi*, a translation of Arnaldo Fortini, *Nova Vita Di San Francesco D'Assisi*, by Helen Moak (New York, N.Y.: Crossroad, 1981).

How truly and innocently the legend-makers had understood! Clare hoped the story would survive the ages and that it would be told around the fire to every son and daughter of Assisi.

It was Francis, however, whom Clare loved above all others. Her own sanctity and clarity of spiritual vision seem to have enabled her to penetrate more deeply than anyone else into the mystery of his extraordinary holiness, and with the miracle of the stigmatization her reverence must have increased immeasurably.

Lothar Hardick, O.F.M.

La Verna

One night when the moon was full and bright over the valley of Spoleto, Clare reached out and held Francis in her soul. He was away to the north at the time on a lonely mountain called La Verna and she felt his pain. He became somehow tangible to her, as if he were there reaching out to her in her cell.

He rested heavy on her mind, and she felt the heat of his cauterized eyes pulsing softly in the darkness. Her silent grief began dropping in tears to the floor. Somehow this moment was more real to her than if Francis were really there. Her whole cell was flooded with light and air while their two souls floated lightly between the moonbeams that held this vision through the night.

Francis' soul seemed so light to her, so small and frail, so different from the power that flowed from him in daylight as he preached or walked magnetically through the streets of Assisi. He always said how small and wretched he was, that in him God had chosen to work through the lowliest of creatures. And now, as she held his spirit in her soul, she knew that it was true. How could this tiny, gentle man, so vulnerable, so sensitive, radiate such power?

And then shortly before dawn she suddenly felt as if a flame had touched her. The spirit within her fragile frame burned with a love hot as a seraph, and she experienced the entry of the living God. Francis far to the north on Mount La Verna was sealed with the wounds of Christ. And it was morning.

A Song for Her

The whole world was present to her at San Damiano. The closer she grew to the one who is love in her small garden there, the more all of creation opened up to her. Clare marveled at how well she knew Mount Subasio simply from so many hours of looking at it in the distance. It had entered inside her and become a part of the way she saw all trees and every mountain. The more intimate her union with God became, the closer she seemed to be to nature, to the other Poor Ladies, and to Francis and his brothers. All these intimacies were somehow one and inseparable.

In the beginning she had feared (though she couldn't admit it then) that the love of God would divide and separate her other loves. In a sense it had, perhaps because she expected it to. But as she grew older and persevered in prayer, she experienced at the deepest level of her being a coming together, a centering of love. She dared to believe that in loving the Lord she had broken through to a more perfect love of nature and of people.

Sometimes, for example, as she was praying before the crucifix and lifting her eyes to the crucified, she would see the face of someone else. At first this experience had frightened her because she thought her love for people might be greater than her love for Christ. Then one day when one of the brothers was preaching in San Damiano, she looked at his face and saw there the face of Jesus. The two had become inseparably joined for Clare.

And she experienced something of God's Spirit in the lives of trees and flowers. The force that drove the flowers up into sunlight drove her to lift up her heart and mind in prayer.

Over the years Clare had wondered if Francis felt this way too, and she prayed that God would reveal this to her before Francis died. The answer came when Clare least expected it. Francis came to San Damiano in the spring of 1224 just after returning from La Verna where Christ had burned his own brand marks into Francis' flesh. He was very weak, and suddenly his eye sickness worsened. As a result he had to stay there for more than fifty days in a little cell next to the monastery.

One night when he was plagued more than ever by pain and sleeplessness, Francis began to feel sorry for himself. He cried out to the Lord to help him bear his suffering patiently. And the Lord answered him, promising him in exchange for his present pain an everlasting treasure beyond his dreams.

The next morning Francis composed his Canticle of the Creatures and set it to music. Clare heard this song with amazement and with a new understanding of Francis. He whose eyes could not bear the light of the sun praised the Lord first of all through the sun; he whose bleeding eyes could not bear the candlelight praised God through Brother Fire who is beautiful and gay, full of power and strength! Clare understood then how close Francis was to creatures. He had chosen this creature world as his instrument of praise of God. And she knew in her heart that he saw her face in Sister Moon for he had dubbed the moon bright and precious and fair—words which Brother Leo once told her Francis used in describing Clare herself.

Then Francis did one of those things which she had come to expect from him. He immediately dictated another canticle with words and music for her and all the Poor Ladies of San Damiano, a canticle full of the wise teachings he had always given them:

Listen, little poor ones called by the Lord,
Who have been gathered together from many parts
    and provinces;

Live always in truth,
That you may die in obedience.

Do not look at the life outside,
For that of the Spirit is better.

I beg you in my great love for you,
That you use with discretion the alms
    which the Lord gives you.

Those who are weighted down with sickness,
And those of you who are wearied by the care of them,
You should all of you bear it in peace,
For you will see that such fatigue is very precious.

For you will each be a Queen crowned in heaven,
    with the Virgin Mary. Amen.

Clare heard these words with tears in her eyes, for
they told her that Francis knew what she was thinking
and was answering her question. He turned her attention
from him back to the Spirit inside, hinting at how he saw
her and each of the Poor Ladies at San Damiano: They
were mirrors of the Virgin Mary herself. What he felt for
them would not be left unsaid until eternity. And Clare
turned in wonder to her garden and to Mount Subasio and
to prayer before the crucifix of San Damiano.

*...[O]nce the realization is accepted that even
between the closest human beings infinite
distances continue to exist, a wonderful living
side by side can grow up, if they succeed in
loving the distance between them which makes
it possible for each to see the other whole and
against a wide sky!*

Rainer Maria Rilke

Brother Sun, Sister Moon

Why was the moon always visible when the sun was shining in Assisi? Even at midday when the sun was at its zenith, you could see the moon as well. "Brother Sun and Sister Moon," Francis had called them. Could he have seen in these two heavenly bodies an image of himself and her? The sun, like God's love shining through Francis, lit up the moon which was Clare; the moon, the eternal symbol of woman. The moon which hangs in heaven lightsome and precious and fair. The moon whose reflection softens the garish radiance of the sun. The sun and the moon complemented each other and belonged together, and in Assisi they hung together in a cloudless sky every day.

This observation confirmed for Clare the rightness of their inseparable partnership in God's Kingdom. And she smiled to think that even a man who took seriously Christ's words about being a light to the world needed a moon to soften and complement God's radiance shining through him. She knew that Francis, too, had realized as much when he sang in ecstasy: "All praise be yours, my Lord, through Sister Moon and Stars; in the heavens you have hung them, bright and precious and fair."

A Fruitful Barrenness

During the great high holy days Clare would think about Francis and celebrate in spirit with him. Christmas, especially, was dear to her because she knew how much that feast meant to Francis. She would see the child Jesus lying in the animals' feeding trough and thank God for this poor Christ whom she and Francis had seen being born anew in their own time. In some way, mysterious but real, she and Francis were there in the nativity scene beside the child, their virginal love so like that of Mary and Joseph that they too gave birth to him and offered him to the world.

That thought made her barrenness fruitful and her virginity precious and warm and soft as a lover's touch. The delicate skin beneath her rough habit would seem fragrant with a sweet perfume, and Clare would feel so beautiful and so loved, and she would remember joyfully that she was a woman.

She no longer had that gnawing homesickness for Francis' presence that had haunted her as an adolescent. She had learned to live apart, united with Francis in the Lord they both loved. Clare had grown out of being in love and into loving. When that actually happened she

couldn't remember, but she always celebrated this new
love, this new level of loving, on the great high holy days
of the Church.

Freedom From Boredom

W hen she looked at women her age living
comfortably and securely in Assisi, Clare
realized that Jesus' love had saved her from
boredom. How that was, it was hard to explain. She was,
after all, enclosed behind cloister walls, and anyone
looking at her life, its routine, its "drabness," would surely
have thought her mad to say her life was free from
boredom.

But everything she was and everything she did was
part of the great adventure God had revealed to her. The
world was being reborn through the preaching and
example of the brothers and the prayer and poverty of the

Poor Ladies of San Damiano. And so everything she did in that poor convent was charged with meaning, and meaning saves one from boredom and even from despair. What a small corner of the world was San Damiano! But from that place, as from the battlements of the most important castle, a message was going forth to the whole world, a message that every person on earth is blessed because Jesus Christ is Lord.

Clare needed only to observe her own companions to see the effect of a life lived wholly for the Lord. There was a radiant joy upon their faces, and they went about doing the humblest of tasks as if they were members of the papal court. The people of Assisi, too, proclaimed the beauty and significance of the Poor Ladies' lives. They came in steady lines to ask their prayers and to have Clare lay her hands upon the sick. The Poor Ladies were never so much a part of the world as when they withdrew from it to dedicate their lives to God.

Even Francis turned to them for the support he needed in his ministry. Every success the brothers had in building up the kingdom of God was inspirited by the prayer of Clare and her Ladies. They were involved in something that stretched beyond San Damiano, beyond Assisi, even beyond Italy itself.

Leaving Home

Her parents. How they suffered when she ran away from home! How Francis had suffered because they, like his father, did not understand, because they believed he had seduced her into following the dream of a madman. Her father, especially, hated Francis, the wild son of Bernardone who had robbed him of his favorite daughter. He was jealous, too, because he knew Clare shared with Francis her inmost thoughts.

Clare suffered for all of those she had to hurt in following the call of her Savior, Jesus Christ. Hurt! There was always hurt, it seemed, from beginning to end. Eventually there had come a sort of truce—at least their grudging acceptance of what she had done. The pain became less severe, a sort of dull ache you grew used to and learned to ignore if there was to be any peace at all.

Francis had suffered so much misunderstanding in his own life that she winced to think she added to his burden. But it was Francis himself who had encouraged her. He made it easier for her to stand against opposition in her response to Christ. When her relatives came to drag her forcibly back home, Clare thought she would die from the pain and rage she saw in their eyes. It was the same disbelieving, wounded look she had imagined in Pietro Bernardone's eyes that day when Francis renounced his father before the bishop and the assembled citizens of Assisi.

She knew she would not succumb, not return with her relatives, but it cut her deeply to cause so much pain and grief. How many sleepless nights she had spent in prayer for their forgiveness; how many times she wondered why following Christ had to be so hard, so full of separation and alienation from those you loved.

And it was only when Ortolana, her widowed mother, came to live as a nun at San Damiano that Clare knew some peace over the pain she had caused. *Some* peace, because she never knew whether her father had forgiven her before he died. Her questioning of her mother about this was always met with vagueness and evasion, and Clare continued to weep for him. The desire for reconciliation was so deep that she longed for heaven where she would finally be able to tell it all to her wounded father and hear him say he understood.

This, too, she shared with Francis. Though he never told her, she knew he mourned his father's pain more than he ever showed. He would walk past his father's house, his eyes filled with tears as he looked up at the fastened shutters behind which the old man sat and brooded and railed his pain to Lady Pica.

Clare and Francis were orphans of sorts, fatherless children crying in the night for attention and love. They were comforted only by a heavenly Father who had called them to himself and who understood better than they that no one ever fully leaves father or mother, even for God. One only separates in time and place; the bond remains forever.

Loneliness

I s there a cure for loneliness? Can the longing of the human heart be assuaged? Only in God, thought Clare, only in God. But how? Was it in loving God alone and closing your heart to others, avoiding risks, cautiously protecting yourself from involvement of any kind? How sterile that seemed, how dangerous—for the risk of not loving is greater than the risk of loving. Clare always refused to believe that the love of God meant withdrawal into oneself. On the contrary, it made possible a new love for others which left no room for loneliness, no time for self-pity.

Loving was always complicated, but *not* loving was even worse—impossible for her. She knew that love was her vocation, a love that embraced everyone and excluded no one. Her life at San Damiano, though relatively hidden and removed, was consciously motivated by her love of God and people. Everything that happened in Assisi was of interest to her because she was intimately involved in the lives of all its citizens, their troubles and their illnesses, their celebrations and their tragedies.

The cure for loneliness was a centering on the God who makes loving possible, then a reaching out to others in self-forgetfulness. Reaching out was beautiful and fragrant like the sweet scent of ginestra on the morning air. That is what it meant to Clare to say that only in God is there a balm for loneliness.

However, it was never just God up there in the heavens nor God in the depths of your own heart who healed you of loneliness. It was also God in the other:

God in the poor, in the leper, in the lonely, in the sick and brokenhearted. Clare tried to teach the Poor Ladies this simple truth lest they withdraw into the luxury of thinking about themselves and God and the terrible selfishness of taking responsibility for no one.

Reaching out meant being responsible for others. If you were a contemplative, your love reached out to the whole world, and you took all the world's pain and suffering and confusion into your prayer and your loving. You were a part of everyone and everything, and you felt in a real way your connectedness with all of creation. Who could be lonely with so many to love, so many to care for, so many needs to present to God? That loving was complicated at times only assured Clare that she was still human, that she was living as a woman instead of some sexless being trying to escape from the responsibility of being involved with humankind.

Loneliness was for the uninvolved, the self-seekers, unless you were in love with God, as Clare was. Then loneliness was really longing, a yearning to be with your beloved. That kind of loneliness would always be with her; it would always be her friend. But the loneliness which was self-preoccupation and self-pampering would always be a stranger in her house.

Longing drew you out; lonely self-pity drove you inwards. So longing was the cure for loneliness, even though the longing of the human heart for God could not be completely satisfied here on earth.

God had called her through Francis to the
literal following of Christ in the way of
the Holy Gospel, and that call was absolute.
It bound her to Francis in a union so close and
so intimate that she saw it under the imagery of
a child fed from its mother's breast.

Lothar Hardick, O.F.M.

A Vision

Clare often dreamed of Francis, but no dream moved her more than one that was more like a vision than a dream. She saw a high stairway, and she was climbing it as lightly as if she were on level ground. She was carrying a jug of hot water and a linen towel to Francis. She was climbing the high stairway quickly, as if she were on level ground. When she finally reached him, he bared his chest and said gently, "Come and drink, my virgin, my Lady Clare." She drank. And afterwards Francis asked her to drink again. And in the dream she drank something so sweet and delightful that she could not find words to describe it. When she drew away from him, a golden nipple remained between her lips. She took it reverently into her hand, and she saw in it everything, as in a mirror.[5]

Over and over again she meditated on the vision and pondered its meaning. Was her relationship with Francis like that of a child fed at its mother's breast? Was he the

---

[5]This vision is recorded in the process of Clare's canonization.

incarnation of Jesus for her, the mediator of Jesus' own living water? Was she drinking of Francis' own spirit? Was his heart the mirror of her own? Or was it all of these together or separately, as she needed?

Whatever the meaning, that vision bound her to Francis anew and made him more present and tangible than if he were bodily before her. That the vision was from God she had no doubt. She received and treasured it as a precious gift from God who understood how important Francis was to her and how intimately her life was bound to his.

Letting Go

T he only thing that kept her going at times was the fact that the *Lord* had brought her to San Damiano. It was not her doing, or fate, or some accident that she met Francis and fell under his spell. It was God's doing. So God would have to determine what it all meant and where it was supposed to lead; it was too much for her.

She wondered how those who didn't know the Lord survived separation from their loved ones or for that matter, how they survived any tragedy at all. And she was grateful once again for faith, for that gift which sustains the heart and gives meaning to the sometime puzzle which is life.

Clare knew she had done nothing to deserve the faith she now had, and she felt an enormous sadness for those who were without it. As difficult as God seemed at times, at least she knew God existed and that God cared. Without God she could never persevere. It was difficult even to imagine life without faith in a living God who loved her and cared about her. And so she continued to put everything into God's hands.

It was the letting-go that had been hardest to give to the Lord. Letting go of her parents, letting Francis and the brothers move away while she and the Poor Ladies remained at San Damiano. Yet she knew that was the only way—the denying, the love that doesn't cling, the heart made pure by giving away, the sharing. And once she had let it go, everything seemed closer to her than ever. It was like that with the Lord. You struggled and wrestled with God for something and when you finally gave in and let go, God gave you freely what you had tried to wrest.

That was the way it had been in her struggle to hold on to Francis. She couldn't remember when or how she let go, but sometime at the very beginning she had released him emotionally and given him back to the Lord. From that day on he was never far from her thoughts, and he was always in her heart. It was the Lord's doing, she was sure, and so she left the whole matter in the Lord's caring hands.

Since God had taken the initiative, she would let God continue to do so. And she would wait upon God's will, she would receive only what and when God was ready to give. She, like God's mother Mary, would wait and store up everything in her heart, trying to be God's handmaid.

That was the hardest test of all: to sit back and wait for God to effect what you would like to take into your own hands and accomplish through your own initiative. But Clare knew that nothing could be accomplished by human effort alone; only the grace of God made anything possible. And so you learned to surrender to God, you learned to acknowledge your own helplessness, you learned that you could not control or be on top of everything in your life.

And once you learned that terrible lesson, everything made more sense. It was easier to let go, to trust, to believe that God would do more for you than you could do for yourself. First you had to wrestle with God, you had to try and beat God and go it alone and end up wounded. Then your surrender meant something. Then you felt that what God gave you as pure gift was something you had fought well to win on your own; you knew the worth of God's gift and the impossibility of acquiring it by your own merits.

Thus it was that Clare had surrendered Francis to the Lord and waited for the moment when God would give him back—a moment which never came. For the Lord had been giving Francis to her all along and not in one dramatic moment.

The Lord had brought them together, and he had kept them together; yet they were separated from one another all their lives. What a paradox that was, how different from what she might have chosen for herself or wrested from God by force.

In the end she realized that what she really wanted was faith. She wanted to keep believing no matter what happened. She struggled with God for that precious gift, she was wounded in the battle, and she was weary and sick at times from fighting. And then one day she realized how strong her faith really was, that without her even realizing it, the Lord had already given her what she was still fighting for. In her struggle with God she had received the great gift of faith.

She believed God knew and understood and cared. She believed Francis and she were one in spirit even though they were separated in body. Most of all she knew with the certainty of faith that in heaven they would know the fullness of each other's love and the fullness of their mutual sacrifice. And she let go and cried for joy and knew the worth of God's free gift.

In infinity already I see the dawn
We shall be united forever in heaven.

Giuseppe Verdi, *Rigoletto*

Death in October

Winters were hard at San Damiano. The lovely mists of summer that made the valley of Spoleto blue against the mountains suddenly turned to wetness and damp, and Clare would feel a chill in every corner of her life. Sometimes the summer mists seemed to freeze in mid-air; just as her life would move from warm, liquid reverie to the sharp, pointed world of crystal. But always there was more sun than not, and Clare praised God for this reminder that summer would come again. Then she would let go and let winter purify her once more.

Clare's greatest letting-go came during that terrible winter of 1226. The winter she had dreaded for so many years began in early October. Though she knew Francis was dying, it all came so suddenly. One day he was alive; the next day the brothers were bringing his lifeless body to San Damiano and she was kneeling down before the bier looking at him whom she loved.

She saw in his hands and feet the marks of the wounds of Christ and in his side the lance-wound as well. She bent over and touched tenderly his wounded side, and she burned with love for him who now watched her from afar—or was he nearer than he had ever been before? She kissed his hands and feet and saw him smiling in eternity.

Clare suddenly felt an enormous sense of waste. How much she could have given him during his life had he let her, had they been different kinds of people. But they weren't, and maybe that was the greatest reason Christ had kissed Francis with his own wounds.

Francis had deprived himself of all womanly love and affection for so many years. Even during those fifty days he lay sick and feverish at San Damiano after descending the mountain of La Verna, he was strong in his resolve to hold her at a distance. She did not apply lotions to his eyes, she did not kiss them; and her heart was sick that he should suffer so much alone without her consoling embrace.

How great Francis' love of God must have been to see in even the smallest intimacy with her a kind of coveting of his Lord's virgin bride. His life had been a constant letting-go, and Clare in turn would let him go. She knew this further letting-go would be hard and that winter was threatening the hillside where she lived. She could not think of that; it was too dark and cold a thought. Instead she looked up at Brother Sun and let Francis go and surrendered, for she knew that she would rise again, even from this...even from this.

Waiting for Eternity

He was gone. Only memories now, open wounds flinching with every thought of him who had been so much a part of all she was and all she loved. Everything seemed to remind her of Francis; sudden bird song from some distant cypress tree, a shaft of sunlight across her cheek, a man's voice on the road outside, a friar walking in the distance. She didn't cry much; she only hurt deep within.

From that day on there was less sunlight for Clare, the song of the birds seemed melancholy and the sky was grayer than she had ever remembered before. She was sick more and her heart began to wait for that union with Jesus in paradise. Whenever she was afraid she was forgetting, she would walk down to the chapel Francis had restored, touch the walls gently and kiss tenderly the cold, smooth stone—and he would be there. For the next twenty-seven years not one day went by that Francis was not with her in prayer.

To others Clare seemed the same. She was always cheerful and giving, ever solicitous for the needs of all the Poor Ladies. But she had turned a lonely corner in her life, and it was twilight inside until she would walk once more with Francis. She knew their lives were so intertwined that they would be united again in heaven.

She longed for heaven. She longed to be with Jesus and with Francis. Heaven was for those who had given everything and everyone away. Heaven was theirs, and heaven gave back what they had given away. In heaven *my* was a good and holy word again, especially for those who wouldn't say it here on earth. Clare took comfort from that thought; and even though the sky turned gray and the sunlight seemed dimmer and the birds sang sadly, she would lift her heavy heart to the heavens and cry inside, "My Lord Jesus, I'm coming to you. I love you. My Francis, lead me again to your Lord."

A Lesson in Love

Francesco, the Frenchman. All his ways had been graced with the courtesy of the troubadours she had seen in her father's house, those French minstrels who knew so much of the science of lovemaking and so little at times of the art of love.

Clare smiled now as she remembered the songs of love she took so much to heart as a young girl. They had in fact, been her dowry of heart and mind until she heard Francis talk of a love that outlasted the song and the melody. From the troubadours she had heard over and over again the formulas of love, the science of making a woman happy. Yet it was Francis who had made her supremely happy. And there was in him not even the shadow of idolatry of her, no trace or hint of infidelity to the Christ he loved above her, above all else that existed. The love of God, he said, transcends all we know of earthly love and yet embraces earthly love and sublimates it into an eternal human love. The meaning of his words, she, who loved him so, had learned through years of deprivation and sacrifice.

Now that he was in heaven, Francis was more present to her and more human than he had been when he walked the streets of Assisi. About human love Clare was sure she had known more than Francis had. But of divine love he was the master, and in the end that love had made him more human than she dared to believe he could become.

That was the mystery of it all, the divine becoming human. It started with Jesus, and Francis made it real again for her and for all his brothers and sisters. How much her Poor Ladies needed to know that very simple truth: If they would become human, they must become divine! Understanding that correctly, without heresy and without the subtle distinctions of the theologians, was her secret from Francis, her gift from her Seraphic Father who had loved God so intensely and perfectly that he ended up loving her. Only one who loves God above all can love a woman as she should be loved, selflessly, totally, with God's own love enfleshed in a poor little man.

A Mountain Man

Not everyone was as safe out there on the mountain as Francis had been, for he was a mountain man and understood its moods. He had known how to make the mountain his friend. The mountain helped to keep away the world and its distractions, to restore his broken spirit when he had been too long on the road, to hide him from those who were taxing his patience and his strength.

For years Clare meditated with her eyes fixed on Mount Subasio. She would imagine she saw Francis up there surrounded by ginestra, lying on his back with his hands behind his head. He would be watching the swallows soaring in the sky high above. There would be larks and smaller birds flitting from bush to bush because they could not fly as high, and Francis would notice them too. He was a mountain man; he knew how to see what was around him.

He loved the storms of Mount Subasio and the fresh odor the olive trees gave off after a short rain when the clouds blew over and the sun came out again. She was sure Francis was never afraid because he and the mountain were friends and one day as he always did for creation, he would sing the mountain's praises when he was old enough to sing them well.

He never sang the mountain song; he died before he knew enough to sing it. But he sang that other song of Brother Sun, and it contained something of what the earth had told him, perhaps everything the earth had told him. Clare knew that most of what he sang about nature he had learned on Mount Subasio. And this is what he sang, this is how he sang it:

Praised be You, my Lord, through all Your creatures,
Especially Sir Brother Sun,
Who makes the day and enlightens us through You,
He is lovely and radiant and grand;
And he heralds You, his Most High Lord.

Praised be You, my Lord, through Sister Moon
And through the stars.
You have hung them in heaven shining and precious
And fair.

And praise to You, my Lord, through Brother Wind,
Through air and cloud, calm and every weather,
That sustains your creatures.

Praised be You, my Lord, through Sister Water,
So very useful, humble, precious and chaste.

Yes, and praise to You, my Lord, through Brother Fire,
Through him You illumine our night,
And he is handsome and merry, robust and strong.

Praised be You, my Lord, through our Sister, Mother Earth
Who nourishes us and teaches us,
Bringing forth all kinds of fruits and colored flowers
And herbs.

It was all there between the lines; so much was said
between the lines with Francis! He had always called her
Lady Clare, and that said more than most people realized.
He sang of a sun that was masculine and a moon that was
feminine, and of wind and fire that were a different sex
from water and earth; that too said more than even she
dared to guess. What goes on in the deep heart of a poet
who praises God through creatures, none of whom are
plant or animal and all of whom rest between a masculine

sun and a feminine earth?

Clare was a woman of the plain, but she too had traveled the mountain, that other mountain of the mind where the elements of the world become the geography of your own soul. You make them your own and praise God through them, for they have become the stuff of your own self, of who you are. You praise God through earth and water and air and fire because that is what you are made of; and if you are a poet like Francis, you know how to pair them and how to describe them and what value they have. Francis had indeed been a mountain man, but he was a poet and mystic too.[6]

The Garden

C lare once again threw open the shutters as when she was a child eager to look down into the Piazza of San Rufino and watch the people bustling about in the gathering rays of the morning sun. But now she looked out into the garden where the roses and gladioli had grown through the night without her. How extraordinary that thought was—what we love and think we care for (and do care for) has a life apart from us. A life which in its most extraordinary and essential aspects takes place apart from us. It is alone in its birthing and

---

[6]This meditation relies upon the ideas of Father Eloi Leclerc, O.F.M., developed so profoundly in his book, *The Canticle of Creatures: Symbols of Union* (Chicago, Ill.: Franciscan Herald Press, 1977).

growing and dying. In Jesus' Mystical Body we are all united as the branches are that cling to the vines of the grape arbors on the side of Mount Subasio. We witness in turn their planting and grafting and withering before the frost. But we do not experience for them that coming to life and growing and suffering and dying. We are then, all of us, joined to everything that is and at the same time alone, apart from everything in our deepest experiences. The plants in the garden of San Damiano grow apart from her though she may tend them and talk to them and seem to watch over them.

Her sisters were like that, too. She could not suffer infection with the Lady Benvenuta nor scrofula with the Lady Andrea. She couldn't be there for them; she couldn't be them, nor be their growing through the night as they slept. She could only open the shutters of her heart at dawn and trust that her sisters, like the roses and gladioli, would be there opening again to the light that illumined their garden. She could pray for them, suffer and rejoice with them. She couldn't suffer their pain, know their joy for them.

Our coming into the world is ours alone to know and feel, that passage from darkness through the narrow canal into the light. Our passing out of this world is ours alone, as well, though others hold our hand and pray with us and flood us with tears that once again moisten our passage with love as did our mother's womb. Even God does not make that passage for us as the Father demonstrated so dramatically in sending his Son to be born of a woman, to live and die like all of us, alone, though surrounded with the Father's love, companioned by his mother and what few friends would stay and watch his lonely passage into the light of the eternal garden.

How strange. She only meant to open the shutters and greet the morning light, touch the flowers and plants with her fingers, and all these thoughts rushed in. They always did, it seemed. Like mirrors of her soul the things of her garden reflected what grew within her and triggered thoughts profuse as petals. How strange. How wonderful.

She lifted her eyes to the sun's rising over Mount Subasio and light flooded her whole being. And once again she blossomed into praise.

The Mirror

"Bring the mirror, Sister Philippa. Quickly. The mirror." And dear Sister Philippa knew. She brought the ciborium with the consecrated hosts. Clare and the assembled sisters fell to their knees before their Lord and prayed aloud Francis' holy words: "We adore you, most holy Lord and Savior Jesus Christ, here and in all your churches which are in the world." Then Clare rose and taking the blessed mirror from Philippa's trembling hands, she went to the door and asked Benvenuta to slide back the lock and open the door. The Poor Ladies gasped at her request, but she was firm and Philippa did as Clare asked.

That was how the mercenary soldiers of the Emperor were driven away. Not only from San Damiano where rape and pillage were all but a certainty had the soldiers entered, but from Assisi, as well. And Clare's only weapon had been the soldiers' mirror. They looked at what she held aloft and like those who see their image again after many years, they recognized the image of everything holy they suddenly remembered from their childhood: their mother's face, her words, their father's face, their church or mosque or temple, the holy books, their own face—the face they recognized was really their own calling them to become who they were in God's eyes. And they drew back in fear and recognition. They saw their God, they saw their own reflection, who they were behind the faces they had donned like masks. And they were afraid and ashamed, as if they'd rushed upon their own mother or father and only recognized them at the final moment when they saw a likeness of themselves in the one they were about to attack.

That was a memory now, but as Clare lay waiting for Brother Leo to bring her the Blessed Host, it seemed like only yesterday. And today it would all be made fresh again when the people of Assisi would come to San Damiano—as they did each year on this day to commemorate the day when the mercenary soldiers retreated—to give thanks to God for the deliverance of their Beloved Assisi. The Perdono, they called it. The Pardon. And so it was.

Memories

S he realized she was no longer young. She lived each day to the full and tried to be wholly present to her prayer and her work, but more and more she noticed herself slipping into memory. And her memories seemed always good. She would remember the glorious days of her youth as she listened to Francis preach, the long honeymoon of those first years at San Damiano and the lovely times when Francis and the brothers would come to share what God had done for them upon the road. It all became lovelier in memory.

This is what it was to be older: You had the memories of ecstasies that the young thought only *they* understood. You, too, had been loved. You, too, had loved and felt the warmth run all through your body; you had run through the poppy fields outside of Assisi and shouted your joy to the sky. Then somewhere in between youth and now you lost it, that vision, that radiant dream of youth—only to rediscover it more tranquilly and more completely in memory's mansion, that peaceful refuge of the aging lover.

Imagination, too, played a part; for Clare felt nothing could really have been so beautiful as the beginning now seemed from the vantage point of a woman fifty-eight years old. As soon as she thought of fifty-eight, she felt strangely young again, for what were so few years, after all, to one who never tired of singing God's praises? At that moment she wanted many more years if only to share the memory of the beginnings with hundreds of women to come. The memory would keep alive the dreams of what life could be if one surrendered wholly to the Lord and shared that life with others. Old age gave hope and wisdom to the young when the memories were precious and pure.

The Legend of Brother Thomas

Clare smiled. She was embarrassed, yet strangely satisfied, because Brother Thomas of Celano had gotten it right, mostly, in this *Legenda* he'd written for Francis' canonization at Pope Gregory's behest. He wrote of San Damiano, he wrote of buildings and gems and Church. All of these, indeed, were right. But then there were other things that...well, she'd read it over again....

"The first work that blessed Francis undertook after he had gained his freedom from the hand of his carnally-minded father was to build a house of God. He did not try to build one anew, but he repaired an old one, restored an ancient one." There was so much there, volumes in Clare's mind about who Francis was and what he did. True, unlike the heretics, he did not try to build a new church, but he did repair an old one, the crumbling chapel of her beloved San Damiano, but something more, too, the Church of the Apostles and Martyrs and Virgins, as well. "He did not tear out the foundation," Brother Thomas wrote, "but he built upon it, ever reserving to Christ his prerogative, though he was not aware of it, for another foundation no one can lay, but that which has been laid, which is Christ Jesus."[7]

Clare lifted her eyes to the crucifix beside her bed and cried aloud, "Yes, Most High Lord, yes, yes, yes." But then she dropped her eyes to the manuscript once more and frowned at the phrase, "though he was not aware of it." Wasn't he? Oh, Brother Thomas, how is it that you know what Francis knew and did not know? Perhaps even then the Most High had already revealed to him that Christ Jesus was the only cornerstone, the only foundation. But then, what did she know? Brother Thomas, so learned, so elegant in his words, God must truly be with his quill, the Holy Spirit guiding his thoughts, even as his beautiful text continued, "When he had returned to the place where, as has been said, the church of San Damiano had been built in ancient times, he repaired it zealously within a short time with the help of the grace of the Most High. This is the blessed and holy place, where the glorious religion and most excellent order of Poor Ladies and holy virgins had its blessed origin about six years after the conversion of St. Francis and through that same blessed man."

And now of her, so unworthy of words that shine as do these of Brother Thomas. "Of it, the Lady Clare, a native of the city of Assisi, the most precious and firmest stone of the whole structure, was the foundation." A stone, Brother Thomas, a stone, but no foundation. Only he whom you have named above, only Christ is foundation of this or any other dwelling within or without. "For when, after the beginning of the Order of

---

[7]This passage is from Thomas of Celano's *First Life of St. Francis* and is translated by Placid Hermann, O.F.M., in *St. Francis of Assisi, Writings and Early Biographies, English Omnibus of the Sources for the Life of St. Francis*, Franciscan Press, Quincy College, Quincy, Ill., 1991, pp. 244-246.

Brothers, the said lady was converted to God through the counsel of the holy man, she lived unto the advantage of many and as an example to a countless multitude." How strange it was to read of oneself as if you were already in heaven. Would that she could be an example to a countless multitude! Instead, here she was, this poor Lady, hidden away in the wounds of the crucified Christ who alone is example, who alone gives advantage. He who, despite Brother Thomas's words, had indeed drawn her to himself before she met Francis, who was bridegroom even before his mirror shone brightly in the Piazza of San Rufino. But then, perhaps that is to quibble, for what Brother Thomas no doubt meant was that Francis drew her to God by a special way in which she, like him to her, was mirror of Lady Poverty. Lady Poverty whom he led her to embrace and who became for her the poor crucified Christ and she the Lady Poverty whom Christ had abandoned in his swift flight in glory after the Resurrection, there to claim the riches which were his from the beginning. For though he was in the form of God, as St. Paul says, Christ did not cling to divinity, but emptied himself, taking the form of a slave, becoming obedient, obedient even to death on the cross.

What is before and what is after in the action of the Spirit of God? It was like asking what came first, the chicken or the egg, in the fable her mother told her as a child. "She was of noble parentage, but she was more noble by grace; she was a virgin in body, most chaste in mind; a youth in age, but mature in spirit; steadfast in purpose and most ardent in her desire for divine love; endowed with wisdom and excelling in humility; bright as her name, Clare, brighter in life, and brightest in character." Oh, Brother Thomas, how swiftly runs your rhetoric! How carried away you become! Like all those whose scribbling quill takes wing its own and outruns the common sense of the one who holds it. If you wish, though, you may indulge yourself, though you know not what only God can know, and God's Most Holy Spirit. I'll grant you this extravagance if only to preserve the truth, the grandeur of what follows. For here indeed the Spirit speaks.

Over her arose a noble structure of most precious pearls, whose praise is not from [humans] but from God, since neither is our limited understanding sufficient to imagine it, nor our scanty vocabulary to utter it. For above everything else there flourishes among them that excelling virtue of mutual and continual charity, which so binds their wills into one that, though forty or fifty of them dwell together in one place, agreement in likes and dislikes moulds one spirit in them out of many. Secondly, in each one there glows the gem of humility, which so preserves the gifts and good things bestowed from heaven, that they merit other virtues too. Thirdly, the lily of virginity and chastity so sprinkles them with a wondrous odor that, forgetful of earthly thoughts, they desire to meditate only on heavenly things; and so great a love for their eternal Spouse arises in their hearts from the fragrance of that lily that the integrity of that holy affection excludes them from every habit of their former life. Fourthly, they have all become so conspicuous by the title of the highest poverty that their food and clothing hardly at all or never come together to satisfy extreme necessity.

Fifthly, they have so attained the singular grace of abstinence and silence that they need exert hardly any effort to check the movements of the flesh and to restrain their tongues; some of them have become so unaccustomed to speak that when necessity demands that they speak, they can hardly remember how to form the words as they should. Sixthly, with all these things, they are adorned so admirably with the virtue of patience, that no adversity of tribulations or injury of vexations ever breaks their spirit or changes it. Seventhly, and finally, they have so merited the height of contemplation that in it they learn everything they should do or avoid; and happily they know how to be *out of mind for God*, persevering night and day in praising him and in praying to him. May the eternal God deign by his holy grace to bring so holy a beginning to an even more holy end. And let this suffice for the present concerning these virgins dedicated to God and the most devout handmaids of Christ, for their wondrous life and their glorious institutions, which they have received from the lord Pope Gregory, at that time Bishop of Ostia, requires a work of its own and leisure time in which to write it.[8]

It was all there. And yet none of it was there, for who could write of that mysterious action of God within each of the Poor Ladies and among them together? That work of God was hidden in God, as were their lives. It would take more than another book and the leisure to write it. It would take the pulling aside of the veil. And only eternity would pull it back.

But Brother Thomas had written beautifully of what he could write. He had done them and all who read his words a service that would edify and inspire them to build anew the Church of the Apostles, the Martyrs and the Virgins, as the Poor Ladies had tried to do at San Damiano.

---

[8]Ibid.

The Consummation

S he remembered the first time she saw the poor
crucified Christ. She was sitting at the window of
her home sewing and absently gazing at the piazza
below just as the first rays of the sun were beginning to
slide across the cobblestones. She was thinking of the Son
of God making his way toward Jerusalem to be handed
over to his enemies. She was wondering what Christ
looked like as he walked steadfastly toward Jerusalem's
gates. Then suddenly, he was there. He wore a tattered
peasant's garb with a rope tied around his waist. He was
barefoot and unkempt, and children were mocking him
and throwing stones at his heels.

Clare leaned out the window and recognized
immediately that it was Pietro Bernardone's son,
Francesco. And now he'd become the Christ of her
imagining. She fell in love with this mirror of Christ she
saw before her; the man himself, as she would come to
know, was a different story. And yet, through the years,
who Francis really was and the Jesus he mirrored became
more and more one, and that is why she loved him. In
Francesco, Bernardone's son, she saw Jesus Christ alive in
Assisi's streets, the Christ we could all become if we
would take the crucifix as the mirror of who we are when
all the poses and masks are removed.

And more than just the crucifix. The whole life of
Christ from crib to cross to empty tomb was the mirror of
the soul made visible in the life of the Savior, Jesus
Christ. She knew it was so. And when she saw Francis and
began to observe him from afar and then more closely, she
knew the life of Christ could indeed be lived in Umbria,

in Assisi 1200 years after Jesus ascended into heaven.

She'd fallen in love with Jesus as a child, she fell in love with Jesus' image when she was eighteen. And Francis continued to call her back again and again to her Bridegroom, Jesus Christ. Whenever she saw Francis or heard of his deeds and those of the knights of Lady Poverty, she would look, as to a beloved's painted image, at the crucifix; and it would seem that the corpus had detached itself and was wandering about Umbria preaching again the Good News.

Always it was Jesus she thought of when she thought of Francis. Jesus, whose bride she had become through Francis' wooing. Jesus' bride. How poor she had to be to be worthy of such a Lord, how much poorer she still had to become.

She knew she must become more completely the Lady Poverty Francis spoke of in poetic figures. As he had reminded her of the poor crucified Christ, she must have been for him the Lady Poverty incarnate. And so it had gone, that journey into the life of Jesus Christ: Francis as Jesus' life re-lived, she as Jesus' mystical bride, the Lady Poverty, who would know Christ's love only in the consummation of the cross—the final poverty of her Bridegroom, the fragrant bed of their love wherein she would be made one with her Bridegroom.

Clare lay back on her straw and longed for that consummation.

She was the princess of the poor, the duchess of
the humble, the mistress of the chaste, the
abbess of the penitent.... Her very life was for
others a school of instruction and doctrine. In
this book of life the others learned the rule of
life; in this mirror of life the others beheld the
path of their own life.

Document of Canonization

A Cache of Letters

I n those who'd come to her at San Damiano, Clare
saw women who were searching for someone and
something to belong to. The something was a family
with common goals and ideals, and the someone was
Christ the Lord. Before they came, they had been a part,
yet not a part, of their families and friends. There was
something inside calling them away, calling them to
solitude and prayer.

Even among those who'd loved them these women
felt somehow different and not really at home. To marry
and settle down was too confining to them; to live alone
was unthinkable. In coming to Clare they realized a new
sense of belonging. At San Damiano their deepest needs
would be met by God and by other Poor Ladies, and they
would be able to give freely of the love within them. They
would be in a place where God came first, where life was
simple, where there were others with whom they could
share their love of God.

Nor was San Damiano the only castle of the Great

King. Others sprang up, one as far as Prague in Bohemia. And the lady of the castle was herself the daughter of an earthly king and queen, Ottokar I of Bohemia and Constance of Hungary. Like Clare's own sister, her name was Agnes and she had been promised in marriage to Henry VII of Germany who married Margaret of Austria instead. Then Henry III of England sought her hand, but Agnes took the hand of Christ.

Agnes had heard of Francis and Clare from the missionary brothers who came to Prague. In 1232 and 1233 she built a church and friary and then a monastery attached to a hospital for the poor. Agnes herself entered this monastery of the Most Holy Redeemer in 1234. There she desired to live with her companions the life Clare and the other Poor Ladies lived at San Damiano. And there she lived out her days.

Clare never met Agnes, but they wrote to one another over the years. In their correspondence they met in the Lord. These letters, those of Agnes and copies she'd made of her own, Clare kept and prayed over, because they contained the very heart of their inner life with the Bridegroom. She picked them up again. She crawled painfully to the dormitory window, reached up and swung wide the shutters. Mount Subasio was flooded with late afternoon light. The water in the garden fountain dripped like a liquid hourglass. The chimney swifts were just beginning to scream as they darted feverishly back and forth across the rooftop.

She opened the packet. She made the sign of the cross and began to read.

Assisi, 1234

1. To the venerable and most holy virgin, the Lady
Agnes, the daughter of the most excellent and illustrious
king of Bohemia, Clare the unworthy servant of Jesus
Christ and the unworthy handmaid of the Cloistered
Ladies of the Monastery of San Damiano, with special
respect commends herself as one subject to all and set to
serve all, and wishes you the prize of happiness.

2. I have heard the most wonderful report of your truly
holy manner of life and conduct. This word has come not
only to me but is spread about generally all over the
world. This gives me great joy in the Lord and I am lifted
up by it. The strong current of this joyful response has
carried not only this far but everywhere to hearten those
who serve Jesus Christ or who desire to serve him. This
has happened because you could have enjoyed pomp and
honor and high place in this world beyond the reach of
anyone else. It was yours, if you had so wished, with full
right to marry the great Emperor, in circumstances that
were in accord with his dignity and with yours. But you
set aside all these things with full intent of heart and
unswerving purpose of soul. You have chosen rather most
holy poverty and spare support for bodily needs. You have
united yourself to a Spouse of more noble lineage, the
Lord Jesus Christ. He will guard your virginity spotless
and untarnished. "Whom when you have loved, you are
chaste; when you have touched, you are purer yet; whom
when you have taken to yourself, you are a virgin." His
power is greater than that of any other; his nobility is
more exalted; his countenance is more beautiful; his love

is sweeter; and his courtesy is more gracious. You are already held fast by his embrace. He has adorned your breast with precious stones and has provided priceless pearls for your ears. He has set you about wholly with jewels that shine with a brightness like the springtime. He has placed upon your head a crown as a symbol of holiness.

And so it is, dear sister, or better I should say, dear lady worthy of great regard and respect, because you are the spouse and the mother and the sister of my Lord, you are signed in most brilliant fashion with the sign of inviolable virginity and most holy poverty. Stand firm in the service which you have undertaken! You have taken a strong position and you have made a courageous beginning in a desire to come to the poor Crucified who for our sake took upon himself the suffering of the cross and thus freed us from the power of the prince of darkness, in which we were held because of the fall of our first parent, and who made peace for us with God the Father.

3. O blessed poverty, which brings eternal riches to those who love and embrace it! O holy poverty—to those who possess and desire you God promises the kingdom of heaven and without doubt eternal glory and a most happy and blessed life. O poverty dear to God, our Lord Jesus Christ, who made heaven and earth and rules them all, who spoke the word and the world was made—it was he who bent down to embrace poverty. He said the foxes have their dens and the birds of the air their nests, but the Son of Man—that is Christ himself—does not have whereupon to lay his head, but bowing his head he gave up his spirit.

It was God of such splendor and such greatness who

entered the womb of the Virgin. It was his choice to be despised, needy and poor in this world so that we who were so very poor and in such deep need and in dire hunger of heavenly nourishment might be made rich in him and possess the heavenly kingdom. Therefore you should respond with full joy of spirit and set no limit to your rejoicing and you should be filled with a mighty joy and in true spiritual happiness because you have chosen to set aside the world rather than to be drawn in quest of its honors. You have large reasons to rejoice because it has been your choice to seek poverty in preference to riches which might be held by human hands in these times. Rather than lay up treasure on earth you have set your treasure in heaven where the rust does not consume it, nor the moth eat holes in it, nor thieves break in and steal it away. Because you have acted thus your reward will be very rich in heaven and you have with full right merited to be called the sister, spouse and mother of the Son of the Father Most High and of the glorious Virgin (Matthew 6:20).

4. I believe very firmly that you know well that the kingdom of heaven is promised by the Lord only to the poor and to them it is given, because when the heart is set on some temporal thing the fruit of charity is lost. It is not possible to serve both God and mammon, because you will either love the one and hate the other or you will serve the one and despise the other (Matthew 6:24).

You know one who is clothed does not dare fight with one who is naked, because he is more quickly brought to earth who offers his adversary something to grasp hold of (St. Gregory, "Homily on the Gospel," II 32-2). You understand also that no one can live in great style in this world and reign with Christ in the other life. You know it is easier for a camel to pass through the eye of a needle than for a rich person to enter heaven (Matthew 19:24). You have cast aside your garments in the form of earthly riches so that you may not be wrenched down in the contest and so that you may walk along the straight way and pass through the narrow gate into the heavenly kingdom. This is a very good bit of business and worthy of praise, to leave behind the things of time in order to possess the things of eternity, to receive a hundred for one (Matthew 19:29), and to possess forever the blessed life.

5. Because of all this I have thought it proper to ask your excellency and to beg of your holiness with humility, but with all the urgency I can muster, and to entreat you in the mercy of Christ to hold fast in his holy service which you have chosen. I beg you to go forward from what is good and to speed on to what is better, to press forward from virtue to virtue, so that he whom you serve with the full yearning of your soul may deign to give you the desired reward. I ask you also in the Lord, with all the power that in me lies, that you in your holy prayer have a regard for me your servant, and a useless one, and for your other sisters here in the monastery, who have such a deep feeling for you. We ask this so that with this kind of help we may merit to enjoy the mercy of Jesus Christ and with you enjoy the eternal vision.

Farewell in the Lord and pray for me!

Prague, 1234

To her who is the Mother Clare, Bride of Jesus Christ, mirror of the Lady Poverty.

This morning at Lauds we prayed with God's beloved David, crying out to God,

> I will keep your commands.
> I call upon you, save me,
> for your commands are the truth.

These words, dear Mother, I joined to yours that swiftly pierced my heart when first I read: "You have united yourself to a Spouse of more noble lineage, the Lord Jesus Christ. He will guard your virginity spotless and untarnished. Whom when you have loved, you are chaste; when you have touched, you are purer yet; whom when you have taken to yourself, you are a virgin."

Oh, Mother, how deep-seeing are the eyes of your soul, for I have often thought how weak I am before my own body with only God's commands to sustain me. The precepts of the law, dear Mother, do nothing but remind us of how helpless we are to fulfill them. As the Apostle Paul says in his letter to the Romans:

> In my inmost self I dearly love God's law, but I can see that my body follows a different law that battles against the law which my reason dictates. This is what makes me a prisoner of that law of sin which lives inside my body.

As for me, I was beginning to think that I should let go of the dream of living chastely, virginally, a life all-given to God. Then the lance of your words pierced my heart, and I knew wherein virginity is made sure: by taking to myself that Virginal Spouse whose love ravishes me, yet leaves me a virgin rapt in Him whose strong embrace is of the soul, all-filling my entire body. In Him I am as in a Light, a star bright as the sun yet not blinding or hurting my eyes; for it is with the eyes of the soul that I see this Light and enter it as if I were entering the very soul that sees it.

How can my soul be both the Light and see the Light? Am I, dear Mother, in my soul so united to Him who is my Spouse that we are one, both Light and Light beheld? Because the Bridegroom is other than I, is in fact God, how do I dare say we are one? I do not say it with my mind and heart, dear Mother, for that indeed is blasphemy, but I experience it in my soul. God is the Light I enter, the Light I become when I enter it. And He Himself says to me, "This is your soul. Behold how beautiful it is!" And when I behold, it is Him I see.

This is too wonderful for me, dear Mother, and it does not correspond to any experience I have in mind or body. Always there is the perceived and the perceiver and they are different, and I know the difference. But when this Lover, whose chaste embrace is Light, leads me into my soul, it is like entering a star that is both entering His embrace all-lightful and entering my soul. And they are one. And when the Light has passed, and I return to my ordinary seeing and hearing, I am changed: I know I do not know what I know of Him with mind or heart; I know Him only with and in the soul, and it stands apart like the sun which is apart from us but by whose light we see all that we see. It is an inner sun, albeit in the heaven within each person all-bathed in the luminous waters of Baptism.

I know this all with certainty, dear Mother, so that if I could no longer think or remember, nor see or hear, I still would know the Bridegroom, Jesus Christ, by the Light that he is, the Light in whom I see and who is the very Light I become to see Him by.

Indeed, dear Mother, it is this embrace of Light who is the savior, Jesus Christ, that preserves the Bride's virginity. For she remembers that embrace, even when mind and heart forget, when eyes and ears do not remember. For she remembers by the very Light who embraces her in her soul made Light by Him who is the Light by which she sees Him.

I do not know if what I've written is the teaching of the Church, dear Mother, ignorant as I am. I only know it is what I've experienced in my soul, and your dear letter gave me the courage to transcribe it. If my poor hand has made words that shape the truth that is bent and crooked, I submit the words and all their shapings and connections and combinations to that straight writing which is the teaching of the Church. Those with knowledge Divine, the Pope and Bishops, successors to the Light's Apostles, they will know how best to untangle and write straight in their telling of that which is known in the Light wherein there are no words.

In Him in whose embrace I am already held fast (to return your own words to me) I leave you. In that embrace, dear Mother, remember your poor sisters of Prague.

Agnes

Assisi, 1253

1. To her who is the half of my soul, and who is also the sacred dwelling place of a very special love; to her who is the illustrious queen, who is the spouse of the Lamb, the Eternal King; to the lady Agnes, who is a most dear mother and sister and who is the most special among all others, Clare, an unworthy servant and a useless servant of the handmaids who dwell in the Monastery of San Damiano in Assisi, sends greetings. Clare wishes for you that you be able to sing the new song before the throne of God and the Lamb and to follow the Lamb wherever he goes (Revelation 14:34).

2. O mother and daughter, spouse of the King of all the ages, I have not written to you as often as I have wished to write and not nearly as many times as my soul desires and your heart too would wish. But do not think for a moment or begin to wonder that the fire of love for you in the inmost heart of your mother has been burning any less sweetly. The principal difficulty lies in the lack of messengers and the clear presence of danger along the roads. But now, when I write in response to your love, I am lifted up in great joy with you and I wish you a full measure of happiness in the spirit, O spouse of Christ! This is my desire for you because, like that other most holy virgin, St. Agnes, you have set aside all the glittering, empty things of this world and you have been espoused in wondrous manner to the spotless Lamb who takes away the sins of the world.

3. She is fortunate who can have part in this holy wedding, so that she with her whole heart fixes her affection upon him whose beauty all the blessed heavenly throngs admire without ceasing. His affection holds one fast; his contemplation is like a breath of new life. His kindness fills one to the brim; his sweetness is in overflowing measure. The recollection of him shines with a soft light. His fragrance revives the dead. The glorious vision of him gives beatific happiness to all the citizens of the heavenly Jerusalem. Now, since he is the splendor of eternal glory and the brightness of everlasting light and the mirror without spot (Wisdom 7:26), O queen, spouse of Jesus Christ, look steadfastly into his mirror every day. See in it every time you look—and look into it always—your own face. This will urge you to vest yourself totally, within and without, with adornments of all the virtues (Psalms 44:10), as becomes the daughter and most chaste spouse of the highest king.

4. In this mirror you will find poverty in bright reflection. You will see humility and love beyond words. You will be able to see this clearly with the grace of God and to contemplate it in its fullness.

Fix your attention first on what has prime place in this mirror, and this is the poverty of the babe who is placed in the manger and wrapped in swaddling clothes. What tremendous humility we find here and what astounding poverty! The king of the angels and the lord of heaven and earth is resting in a manger. In the center of the mirror consider long and carefully the humility which walks side by side, with blessed poverty, and the countless labors and hardships which he bore for the redemption of the human race. And, finally, in studying the last features of the mirror, open your mind and your soul to the unspeakable love which prompted him to want to suffer on the gibbet of the cross and there to die the shameful kind of death. Let us give our full attention to what the same mirror, placed on the wood of the cross, sets before the eyes of all who pass by: "Oh all you who pass by the way, attend and see if there be any sorrow like my sorrow." Let me answer with one voice and one spirit him who calls out and laments: "I recall in my soul and my heart grows faint within me" (Lamentations 1:12 and 3:20). When you respond in this way each time you will be caught up more mightily in the circle of love, O queen of the heavenly king.

5. Take a long, loving look also at the delights which cannot be described in words and which he brings to you, and the riches, and the honors that have no dateline to end them. Responding to the greatness of all this, with all the fullness of desire of which your heart is capable and all the love that it can summon, shout out in joy: "Draw me! After you we shall run in the odor of your ointments, heavenly bridegroom! I shall run, lest I faint, until you lead me in to the storeroom, until your left hand is under my head and until your right arm will happily embrace me, and you will kiss me with the most joyful kiss of your mouth." When you are so wrapt in contemplation, think of me, your poor little mother, and remember that I have the thought of you sculpted deeply on the tablets of my heart. There you are dearer than anyone else in the world.

Farewell, dearest daughter, and a farewell to your daughters, unto the throne of glory of the great God, and pray for us! The Friars who bear this letter to you are very dear to us. Brother Amato, loved by God and men, and

Brother Bonagura, in as much as I am able, I do by this present plea commend to your charity. Amen.

Clare paused from her reading.

Look into that mirror. Does this mean that on the deepest level we are to be conformed to the Passion of Christ? And is that Passion the mirror of who we are now? And does that mean that our present conformity to the Passion is the pledge of our future conformity to the Resurrection of Christ? Is this process, then, sequential like time and then eternity afterwards?

Clare wondered. Was it not, this Passion and Resurrection, something that happened in us simultaneously? In our deepest conformity to the Passion were we not most deeply conformed to the Resurrection? It seemed to her that when she was most experiencing in her own life the Passion of Jesus she was simultaneously rising with him. She experienced the Resurrection in her surrender to the crucifixion and death of Christ. In dying she rose, in surrender her life was given back to her. She need not wait for eternity to experience the Resurrection. Eternity was now in her conformity to the poor crucified Savior.

In her illness, in her greatest poverty, she was richer than she'd ever been. In her illness she knew most

intimately the poor crucified Christ, who rose continually
within her, making his own Resurrection real for her in
the image and reality of her own suffering mirrored in him
who came to her not glorified but crucified again and
again as he was in every Mass.

The Mass. That too was for her a further image of the
poor crucified Christ pouring himself out for us by
reenacting the very Passion that is the mirror of our own
suffering and pain. It all became Resurrection when it
became mirror, when Mass and meditation on the crucifix
became the mirror of herself. It was then that she
experienced most deeply the words of St. Paul: I live no
longer for myself, but Christ lives in me.

Clare no longer needed a bronze mirror like the one
she looked into as a girl in her home beside San Rufino.
The crucifix and Mass were the mirror of who she was, of
who she had become.

She turned to Agnes's final letter.

Prague, 1253

My heart overflows with love, dear Mother,
that you have written to me, your
      unworthy daughter in the Poor Christ.
Heeding the words of the Apostle Paul,
    I was bent on keeping my eyes
        fixed on the Lord Jesus Christ
but was troubled how I should follow
    this command and what it might mean,
        when your letter arrived

by the hands of Friars Amato and Bonagura.
How can I fully express my surprise and joy
    when, opening your letter, my eyes fell
        on these fragrant words:

"O queen, spouse of Jesus Christ, look steadfastly into his
mirror everyday. See in it every time you look—and look
into it always—your own face."

Then, dear Mother, I knew what was mine to do:
        Solely to look into that mirror!
    And first at hand was a small crucifix
that graces the poor warm walls of our enclosure.
        Warm with love of God, dear Mother,
    not with that fire outside which burns
        but cannot enlighten the soul.
Then taking that crucifix off the wall
        and kissing it all-reverently
for love of Him whose image it strives to be,
        I thought of the artist
    who made this wondrous crucifix.
        I know him well, dear Mother,
a man who was carver to that court of vanity
    which once I strove to adorn.
        He made of wood fair images
    to grace the sleeping chamber
        I then called my own. But when,
hearing the Savior's whisper at my pillow,
    I left that vanity of velvet and satin
        (and other images more fair
    than what they strove to imitate)
this goodly artist made for our new wedding chamber

an image to fire the walls
with that Passion which suffers that it might
   enkindle and enlighten a love
    that burns away our passions
while stirring up true love all-holy.
What was it, dear Mother,
   in this most simple crucifix?
I must confess it was the artist's hand
   that first met my senses:
the pressure of his tool cutting
long deep lines into the length of wood he broke
   from an almond tree when he was in the Holy Land
    in the Emperor's retinue, the last Crusade.
     Those strokes and gouges, dear Mother,
      reminded me of the Divine Artist
who made these marks upon his Son in the flesh.
   These same marks (like those upon
    St. Paul and our holy father Francis)
speak to us of what love means when it is
   stripped of the vanity that veils it in
silk which tries to belie its true countenance.

Forgive me, Mother, if my poor words begin to
   teach you who know much more than I
    the nature of true love mirrored
     in the Savior's countenance.
   But it is your very words that have inspired
    these words upon the scroll.
   It was your letter, dear Mother, that enabled me
    to see our crucifix for the first time,
     though I had looked often,
but seen only with the eyes of the flesh and not
    with eyes like yours

which are in truth the eyes of a soul
wed to him whose image you behold
as does a bride her beloved
(gone alas, wherever it is men go from those
they've taken to themselves).
Though our dear Savior in being man
does indeed abandon us, in being God
he remains within, more really
than any image can depict.
Most of the time we do not feel his presence,
even as we believe he is within.
And so we need these goodly images,
like this most precious crucifix.
They bring to mind and memory
what dwells within but has no shape or form,
but being Spirit, is the shape of the person
in whom the Spirit dwells.
And so it is, dear Mother, that I look upon
this wooden crucifix
for an image of him who fills my body and soul
giving me the shape and form of him I look upon.
What is it then that I see outside
which also deep within me dwells?
More than anything, dear Mother, I see
how passionately the Savior loves us.
Like doves resting on a sea of milk
are his eyes upon us.
And like some Knight Divine he gives
his body over to torture
that we might see the proof of what he gladly does
to win our hand in Holy Matrimony.
Nor can I look into that mirror, dear Mother,
without seeing myself,

as you so kindly reminded me.
    I am the milk white sea
whereon the gentle doves of his eyes rest.
And how reluctantly I feel those blue-gray doves
    I've seen floating upon the moat
of any castle I have lived in.
Do doves float like geese, dear Mother? Or is it
    only when they find their Savior's face
    and rest thereon as eyes?
Is it then we see them floating on a milk white sea
    that is the Savior and our soul, as well,
    when we look upon him?
Or do I strain too much to say what best is left
    unsaid in that secret bridal chamber where
    we know our Savior's all-virginal,
    though passionate embrace?

It is your letter, dearest Mother, that emboldens me,
    commanding as it does, that I
    look upon the Mirror, Jesus Christ.
    And I, all-eager to obey, took what was
    the closest at hand, that goodly crucifix
    which now I see I have but hinted at.
    I read your words again and turn to
    my Savior's image wrought in wood.
Enough that I but look upon his body, tree-like
    in its twisting love reaching for
    the soil my soul becomes
    because he graciously allows it to.
    Lost in that fair tree and it in me
    I grow silent, yet obedient.
    I do what you, dear Mother, command.
      I look.

I need not say what I see there
except to him upon whose leavéd countenance I gaze.

Remember me to him whose roots now
fasten in my soul.
Your devoted daughter, the humble soil of Jesus Christ,
the sea grown calm beneath his dove-like
resting eyes.

Agnes[9]

The light was waning now. The sky was filled with swifts.
Clare closed one of the shutters and moved painfully to
her straw mat. She lay still and listened for the dove that
came each night to sit in the half-opened window, his
coos singing her to sleep.

---

[9]The letters of St. Clare to St. Agnes of Prague are authentic. Those from Agnes
to Clare are the author's imaginative creations. The translation of Clare's letters
is the translation of David Temple, O.F.M., contained in the 1979 edition of
Clare, A Light in the Garden. cf. Appendix A for the remaining two letters of
Clare.

*Clare strove by perfect poverty to be made like
the Poor Crucified, that no passing thing of
earth might separate the lover from the Beloved
or hinder the course of her union with God.*

Thomas of Celano

Dreams Are for Sharing

Dreams are for sharing. Sharing dissolves the
loneliness of the dream's pursuit and clarifies its
meaning. Her nature was brightness, was light,
and perhaps that was why Francis had invited her to share
the vision Christ had shown him. And she had kept the
light of his dream shining through all the darkness of the
years, a darkness that descended after Francis' death.

The brothers had depended so heavily on Francis to
keep their own dreams alive that when he died, the
brotherhood was split into factions over the meaning of
his dream of poverty. She knew what that poverty was,
that it was something new and untried, that she and
Francis and their followers had stood against all the
conventional life-styles of the Church and insisted on the
practicality of their way of life. And the Pope himself had
approved the poverty of Francis.

Why then was there so much disagreement over
poverty and so much darkening of this new light that had
dawned upon the world? Wasn't it because something else
had died out? Poverty, after all, was not the light of the
world, and it was not poverty that Francis loved above all
else. Always it was Jesus Christ, his suffering Lord and

Savior, who was the Light. It was Jesus he loved and his poverty that Francis embraced.

Why couldn't the brothers see that it was Jesus who had died out in their hearts? They had unwittingly replaced him with an idea, the idea of poverty. How sad it is when the love of the Lord dies out in the human heart, the mind replaces God with an idea to be lived, and how different that is from a person to be loved! Francis had loved and followed the poor Jesus. It was as simple as that, and no amount of arguing could tell you how to do that or define the limits of loving or being poor.

And so she fought to keep the light of love shining on the poor crucified Christ. If they would only keep him before their eyes, the rest would follow. But that is precisely what so many couldn't do. She wondered sometimes if Francis had in fact replaced Jesus in their minds. Dreams are for sharing, and the dream she and Francis had shared was the literal following of the Christ of the Gospels. They had had to follow him by the light of their own hearts and minds illuminated by the Spirit and the Church. The brothers would have to do the same. Arguing was not sharing the dream, nor would disputes over poverty ever illumine the darkness left when the love of Christ dies out in the human heart.

The Privilege of Poverty

U nbarring the locked door and sneaking out at night and stealing down to the Portiuncula in the moonlight, the wind nervously shaking the tiny olive leaves. The brothers waiting on the road with torches in their hands, their faces flushed by the flames, and Francis clipping her hair and the yellow locks falling lifeless onto the dirt floor. The disappointment and pain of having no home and then Francis bringing her to San Damiano and the joys of the Poor Ladies there in that precious little church that Francis himself had restored and their happy life there where everything was poor. Her battle with the Pope for the privilege of living in complete poverty and now his giving in and the announcement that he was this day to secure for her and the Poor Ladies the privilege of poverty forever...

Toward the end it all got mixed up in her mind.

It had taken more than forty years for that to happen. But now as she lay in bed with the fragrance of Sister Death in the air, it all danced at once in her mind, and her whole life was like a day, a moment of celebration.

Clare looked at the bare ceiling of the dormitory. Her eyes wandered wearily over the plain stone walls, and it all became a palace of poverty, a rich simplicity that she had spent her whole life preserving. She tried not to be possessive even of this impoverished place, for it was a place, after all, and her Lord and Savior Jesus Christ had no place to lay his head. Even from San Damiano she must be as detached as Francis was, for even the poorest place can become a rich possession for one who has nothing. Clinging to San Damiano was especially dangerous because of its association with Francis and the brothers and the beginnings when she and Agnes and the first Ladies had embarked upon the life of gospel poverty.

And then the swallows who nested in the rafters of the ceiling began to fly in and out singing their excitement in the morning sun, and she remembered how Francis had always returned to the Portiuncula. It wasn't so much a place as a nest, a womb, a center where God had spoken, a source of renewal for the spirit. San Damiano was a sacred space where Lady Poverty lived. There you moved in her presence easily, warmed at the hearth of silence and renunciation, if God so willed. Clare would go wherever the Pope sent her, but wherever she went she would take Lady Poverty with her, and around her and the Poor Ladies would grow another holy space where the poor Christ would dwell.

She closed her eyes with effort, even that simple movement taxing her waning strength. She slept and the dreams kept rushing in. The dreams of memory.

Mercenary soldiers were in the courtyard again and she was shakily holding the ciborium in the open door. The quizzical looks on their faces, the horses pawing the ground, their nervous neighs charging the tense atmosphere, and her prayers to the Eucharistic Christ and their panic and retreat as if from their own mirror. And fire filled the sky over the Portiuncula and she saw herself and Francis and the brothers eating a meal in the open. She was listening to Francis and speaking with him and the word Jesus flew back and forth. It increased in speed and it caught fire and she and Francis were all light and the Seraphim beat the air with hot wings and the breath of God warmed the whole valley....

She felt something at her wrist. She painfully lifted her eyelids and the room was on fire. At the foot of her straw mat stood one of the brothers, and in his hand he held the confirmation of her Rule of Life and the Privilege of Poverty from Innocent, the Vicar of Christ. She took it weakly in her open palm and its strength drove her hand to her heart and she slept.

Last Will and Testament for Saint Clare
and the Poor Ladies of San Damiano

I, brother Francis, the little one, wish to
follow the life and poverty of our most high
Lord Jesus Christ and of His most holy mother
and to persevere in this until the end, and
I ask and counsel you, my ladies, to live always
in this most holy life and in poverty.
And keep most careful watch that you never
depart from this by reason of the teaching
or advice of anyone.[10]

A Burnished Mirror

She held the burnished bronze so that the morning light reflected from its surface onto the crucifix that hung above the cot where she lay. She looked into the mirror's center and saw the crucifix. She looked at the crucifix and saw her own reflection. Christ was in the mirror. She was in the crucifix. Crucifix and mirror were both in her. She was herself the mirror.

Of course she could be seeing it the way she wanted to and coloring it with the glory of this new vision of how it was with them. Be that as it may, what she saw she now saw clearly. They had come to know Jesus Christ in looking upon the mirror of his life as they heard it painted in the Scriptures, in the homilies of their brothers, in their own mirrored lives and ultimately in the Mass. For

---

[10]Translation by Regis Armstrong, O.F.M., in *Clare of Assisi: Early Documents* (Paulist Press, 1988).

it was the Mass that most perfectly mirrored the life of Christ and in that mirror they saw reflected their own lives and they came to discover who they were by living the life of the Poor Christ together at San Damiano.

But it wasn't till now as she held the Privilege of Poverty in her hands that she was sure everyone would know who they had become, who they were, these women who'd lived together for more than forty years. This was the mirror of life they came to know in gazing on God's mirror, the crucified Savior Jesus Christ.

Like mirrors catching each other's images, the crucifix, the Poor Ladies, the Privilege of Poverty all repeated each other's image in one another indefinitely. To remove any one of them took away the image of the other. That's why she wanted this final mirror so. The crucifix and Poor Ladies were not enough. They needed one more mirror to complete them, the Privilege of Poverty, to perpetuate their alternating images. As with the Blessed Trinity, three were one, were continuing generation.

But are not the images reproduced by mirrors illusory? Are they not merely multiplied reflections of a single reality? Of course, she thought. And that reality is God, is the Trinity, one in three. That reality alone is. All else is reflection, as in the Poor Ladies, the crucifix, the document she held in her hands. And is not the reason we are here to reflect the Godhead, the Trinity of three Persons in One? For that Trinitarian reflection was not complete until the Privilege of Poverty was written down by His Holiness, the Vicar of Christ. That validation was like the gift of the Holy Spirit validating the Son and the Father he came to witness to. All was one in the end. All the reflections, the images, were reproduced from the image of the cross.

Clare wondered how long she had realized how important the Pope's validation of their way of life was for more than just the future of the Poor Ladies of San Damiano. It was more than simply a pledge for the future, a guarantee that their way of life would continue. It was the Church's seal on who they already were, on how they'd lived their lives from the beginning. It was the Church saying yes to what they'd lived all along—even when they had other Rules imposed upon them. Dear Gregory IX's Rule. Gregory, who'd been their beloved Cardinal Hugolino. Gregory, who canonized Francis, who commissioned Brother Elias to build the basilica in which Francis' body was buried, who had Brother Thomas of Celano write a *Legenda*, a life of Francis. Cardinal Hugolino, who loved them so dearly, yet who was so dense when it came to gospel poverty's true prerogatives. He'd given the Poor Ladies what amounted to a Benedictine Rule which they lived to the letter, while they continued to live more than that Rule.

It was that "more" which Clare and the Poor Ladies had lived uniquely in the Church and which the Church had finally seen and incorporated into the number of authentic ways of imitating Jesus Christ, of becoming an image of the Poor Crucified Savior. Innocent III had given her this Privilege of Poverty, which Hugolino promptly revoked when he became Pope Gregory IX.

For forty years Clare had held steadfast to poverty's ultimate prerogative: the right, the privilege, to own nothing in this world, to be supported wholly by the begging of the brothers and the alms of God's people, while the Poor Ladies worked with their hands for whatever daily sustenance their own labors afforded them.

The Privilege of Poverty was the final mirror to hold up to the crucifix and to their lives. And now she held it in her hands. Pope Innocent IV, Christ's Vicar, had finally seen who they were, why they were different in the Church, how they mirrored something essential of Jesus Christ.

Who they were and how they'd lived gave meaning to everything in their lives. Clare had articulated that meaning which she'd held close in the cloister of her heart. She'd written down who they were, because she knew how careless people can be of words. She'd heard it in some of the brothers' preaching when they'd said things she was certain were coming from some prejudice or mood or disappointment within and not from a careful, prayerful meditation on God's Word. They'd even made God's Word mean something other than what it said. If human beings, then, could manipulate the Word of God, what would others do to their own words, the Poor Ladies of San Damiano? The Pope's approval, his official sanctioning of their words, would at least minimize their careless interpretation by others who would deprive the Lady Poverty of her right to live forever at San Damiano.

And here it was, that sanction, that seal. The Pope had finally signed her Rule in Jesus' name and handed it back to her, a burnished mirror of the life of the Poor Ladies of San Damiano.

The holy virgin turning to herself began
to speak softly to her soul: "Go forth
without fear, for you will have a good escort on
your journey. Go forth," she said, "for
He who created you has sanctified you.
He has protected you always as a mother does
her child, and has loved you with a tender
love." Then she added, "Blessed be you,
my Lord, who have created me!"

Thomas of Celano

Sister Death

Clare knew she was dying and she couldn't believe how much like life it was. She had known physical and mental suffering for so many years that this new experience seemed like meeting an old, familiar friend. She welcomed Sister Death because she had no fear of her, because it was Sister Death who would bring her into life. It was Sister Death who would return Francis to her at last and bring before her eyes the Lord Jesus whom she had loved with all her heart and soul. This was not death, as other people knew death: an impersonal "it," bringing separation and pain. This was life; all those years of separation from her Lord were that impersonal death which others feared so much and tried so hard to postpone.

Her sisters were around her now. And what was this? Here were Brothers Angelo, Leo and Juniper, her faithful friends. They had become even more dear to her after

Francis' death, and she remembered now that she had sent for them to read the Passion of Jesus to her on her bed of pain. They had come to watch one hour with her.

Leo knelt and kissed the straw of her mat; Angelo consoled everyone, as usual; and Juniper began reading the Passion of the Lord in his inimitable, enthusiastic manner. Clare listened with great peace and joy, and then she said to all in the room, "Do you not see the King of Glory? Here he is before me."

She never knew if they saw the Lord or not, for she was caught up in the vision before her. Then the mother of Jesus entered the room and took Clare into her arms and carried her into heaven. And the light in the garden flamed high, the fire of its passing warming Assisi forever.

...And so I end where I began, in your dormitory, Clare, kneeling now and staring at the flowers someone has placed on the spot where you closed your eyes and opened them again in eternity. I've been transfixed by memories and imaginings, mostly of you and Francis and how your love for him grew from infatuation to a love that surrenders your beloved Francis to his real love and yours: the poor, crucified Savior, Jesus Christ. In the poor Christ on the cross you saw the mirror of Francis, and of yourself, and your sisters, and all who fall in love with God. That broken body, vulnerable, nailed to the

rough wood, unable to strike back, defend itself, became the image of who we must become if we would rise radiant in glory to enter the bridal chamber of the heavenly Bridegroom, Jesus Christ.

That transformation, that movement from looking upon Francis as model to looking upon Christ crucified as mirror is itself the mirror of your life. My own poor imaginings are not deep enough or pure enough to see that final transformation as clearly as the beginnings when Francis filled your thoughts, drew your heart as friend and father, brother and companion without whom you could not imagine how you would make it through this vale of tears and tribulation.

I look at these white gladioli that rest on the floor where you laid your head, St. Clare. Somewhere in their heart is the secret center, the intimate love between you and the Divine Bridegroom of your soul. I see the flowers. I cannot see the center, though I know it's there. These scribblings of mine are about the petals. Someone else will see inside and write the story hidden from one whose imagination fails just there where the deepest mystery begins.

> "Poca favilla gran fiamma seconda:
> forse di retro a me con miglior voci
> si pregherà perché cirra risponda."

> ("A great flame follows a small spark:
> perhaps after me prayer will find a better voice
> so that Cyrrha may respond.")

Dante, Paradiso, Canto I

APPENDIX A

Note: St. Clare wrote four letters to St. Agnes of Prague. The following are the two remaining letters not contained in the narrative of *Clare, A Light in the Garden.*

Assisi, 1235

1. To the daughter of the King of Kings, to the handmaid of the Lord of Lords, to the most worthy spouse of Jesus Christ and therefore the queen and the lady noble beyond compare, Agnes, Clare the useless and unworthy handmaid of the Poor Ladies, wishes health and power and the will to live always in the highest poverty.

2. I give thanks to the giver of all grace from whom every best gift and every perfect benefit, as we believe, comes forth (James 1:17). I wish to render him thanks that he has adorned you with so many titles of virtue and has made you shine forth with signs of perfection which is so great. This has brought you to the point that, having been made a diligent imitator of the Father, who is perfect, you have merited to become perfect, so that his eyes see in you nothing that is imperfect (cf. Psalms 138:16).

This is that perfection which will lead the king himself to seat you with him in the heavenly bridal chamber where he sits in glory upon a throne of stars. He will wish this because you have counted as of less worth the dizzy heights of a kingdom of this world and you have set down as of not so great amount the offers of an imperial marriage. You have rather been one who has sought out most holy poverty in a spirit of great humility and burning charity and in this way you have followed fast in the footsteps of him to whom you have merited to be joined in a true wedding.

117

3. Now I know very well that you are set about by many virtues and I would not want to deluge you with many words and certainly not with unneeded ones. I also know that nothing will be accounted superfluous by you if you can draw some consolation from it. But I must say this one thing, because only one thing is necessary, and I do want to admonish you by the love of him to whom you have offered yourself as a holy and pleasing sacrifice (Romans 12:1) that you be mindful of what you have set before you and that in this you be like another Rachel (Genesis 29:16 ff). This will mean that you will not want to forget the point of your beginning, and that you will hold what you have, that you will do what you do, that you will not allow anything to grow slack. I wish to urge you to pass with care along the way of the beatitudes; that you be sure of step and joyful of heart and quick in response; that you walk with quick pace and light step so that you will not slip along the way nor allow your feet to become laden with dust. Have nothing to do with any who would stand in your way and would seek to turn you aside from fulfilling the vows which you have made to the Most High (Psalms 49:14) and from living in that perfection to which the Spirit of the Lord has called you.

4. Now, in order that you may walk the way of the commandments of the Lord with greater security, follow the counsel of the venerable father, our brother Elias, the Minister General. Place this ahead of the advice of others and reckon it as dearer than any other gift. If anyone tells you anything else, or if someone has something different to suggest to you which will in any way block the way to perfection for you, or which in any manner runs contrary to the vocation which you have received from God, it may well be that you should show him respect but don't do what he says. You have one aim: as a poor virgin to embrace the poor Christ (*pauperem christum virgo pauper amplectere*). Keep your eyes fast on him who for you was reckoned of no account and let your part be to be willing to be held of no account for him. Your spouse is he who is of comeliness beyond all the sons of men (Psalms 44:3), and who for your salvation became the least of men and despised and

118

smitten and wounded in all of his body and dying under the hard requirements of the cross. It is him you want to see (intuere), to gaze upon fixedly (contemplare), and with desire to imitate (imitari).

When you suffer with him, you will reign with him; when you grieve with him, you will rejoice with him; when with him you die on the cross of harrowing demands or bitter circumstances, you will possess a heavenly dwelling place in the splendor of the saints; your name, written in the book of life, will be glorious among all. And, because you have done this, in place of the passing things of this earth, yours will be, for eternity and for ever and ever, the glory of the heavenly kingdom. In place of goods that perish yours will be the things that are eternal and you will live for ever and ever.

Farewell, dearest sister and lady also because of your union with the Lord, who is your spouse. Be sure to commend to the Lord in your devout prayers both me and my sisters who are so very happy about the good things which by his grace he is bringing about in you. Remember us in every way also to your sisters.

Assisi, 1238

1. A greeting in Christ to our sister Agnes, a lady to be held in most high regard, and one of great goodness, and worthy of love from all the people of this earth. Clare, the lowliest of all and the unworthy handmaid of Christ and the servant of the Poor Ladies, sends this greeting to her who is the sister of the king of Bohemia and who is now also the sister and spouse of the most high king of heaven. To her may the author of salvation give the joys of salvation and whatever good and best thing her heart might desire.

2. I am filled with great joy because I know full well that you have gone forward with sure step and have advanced to a happy state of achievement and have won many a laurel on the course which you set for yourself to obtain the heavenly prize. I

breathe with a new sense of high joy in the Lord because I know and just as certainly that, by your intent following in the footsteps of the poor and humble Jesus Christ, you make up in wondrous manner what is lacking on my part and on that of the other sisters.

In all truth I can in full measure respond in joy, nor is there any one who can take this joy from me. I have good reason for this because I possess that which I most desire to have under heaven. And I see how you have thwarted the designs of him who is the most cunning enemy and you have allowed no place for pride which devastates the human person. As I very plainly see, you have with almost terrifying thoroughness and an unexpected swiftness, as if you had just received a wondrous work of wisdom from the mouth of God, set aside the vanity which puffs up human hearts and leaves them empty. You have chosen to seek the treasure with which none other can compare (Matthew 13:44). This is hidden in the field of the world and of human hearts. By buying it you are able to possess him by whom all things were made out of nothing and to embrace him in humility, in the virtue of faith and in the arms of poverty. To use the words of the Apostle (1 Corinthians 3:9), by the judgment of God himself you are the helper and one who lifts up the languishing members of the ineffable Body of Christ.

3. Who is there then that would suggest to me that I should not rejoice over so many causes for joy which also prompt us to imitation? And you also, my dearest one, want always to go forward in joy in the Lord: Do not let bitterness wrap itself around you like a cloud, O most dear lady of the Lord, who are the joy of the angels and the crown of your sisters. Set your mind on the mirror of eternity. Direct your soul to the splendor of glory. Fix your heart on the image of the divine substance. By contemplation transform yourself totally into the likeness of divinity itself (Hebrews 1:3; 2 Corinthians 3:18). Then you will feel what those who are friends feel when they taste a hidden sweetness, which God himself from the beginning has reserved for those who love him (Psalms 30:20; 1 Corinthians 2:9). In this manner you pass quickly by all those things which in this

topsy-turvy world with all its false lights hold fast many who are ensnared in a love that is a kind of blindness. Then you are free to love completely and totally him who gave himself totally for love of you. The sun and moon shine in wonder at his greatness (Divine Office of St. Agnes). There is no limit to the abundance of his rewards nor to their values or their greatness. He it is who is the son of the most High, whom a Virgin bore and after childbirth remained a virgin. Stay close to his most sweet Mother who bore so great a son, whom the heavens could not contain, and still she bore him in the narrow cloister of her womb and as a virgin gave him birth.

Who would not shrink in horror from the snares of the enemy of the human race, who by the proud pretense of brief and tinsel glory strives to bring to naught what is greater than heaven itself?

4. So, dearest of creatures, we know clearly by the grace of God that the soul of a faithful [person] is greater than heaven. We understand this to be true because the heavens with all other created things together cannot hold the creator so that the soul of one of the faithful is alone his dwelling and his seat and this is brought about solely through love which the wicked do not possess. It is the truth who tells us this: "If any man love me, he will be loved by my Father, and I will love him, and we will come to him, and make our abode with him" (John 14:21). Just as the virgin of virgins who was so glorious bore him corporally in her womb, so also you who follow her footsteps can, especially by your humility and poverty, in a chaste and virginal body bear him spiritually. Then you possess him of whom you are more sure in possession than you can be in having for your own anything else in the world. There have been kings and queens of the earth who have spun their own dreams in pride and had plans for taking over the heavens, and they walked with their heads in the clouds. But in the end it all came down as rubble and was piled up as trash.

5. Now, about these things concerning which you asked, I should respond to your loving request. You wanted to know

what are the feasts which our most glorious father St. Francis instructed us to celebrate and especially about the manner of partaking of food on these days. I give it as a counsel to your prudence that first he directed us to use suitable discretion in providing for those who are weak and sick and to have for them whatever kinds of foods will serve their needs. For the rest of us who are well and strong meals for fast days are to be provided, because we fast every day, whether it is ferial or festive. Exempted from these are the Sundays and the Nativity of Our Lord; on these days we are permitted to eat twice. On Thursday, in the usual times, according to the choice of each one, no one is bound to fast. But we who are strong fast every day except Sundays and Christmas. But on every Pasch, as the writings of blessed Francis say, and on the feast of holy Mary and the holy Apostles we are not bound to fast, unless the feast day falls on Friday. But as we mentioned before, we who are strong and healthy always eat only Lenten meals.

6. However, since flesh is not cast of bronze, and since our strength is not that of a stone, and because we are fragile by nature and subject to all manner of bodily weakness, I beseech you, dearest one, to leave off any indiscreet and impossible austerity in abstinence. I beg you in the Lord that with good prudence and a large measure of discretion you withdraw from overexacting austerity into which, as I know, you had plunged yourself. I ask this so that you may be alive to praise God and so that you may render to him a reasonable service (Romans 12:1). So your sacrifice will be seasoned with the salt of prudence. May you fare well in the Lord, so indeed I greatly desire your good wishes for me. I commend myself and my sisters to your holy prayers.

APPENDIX B

Chronology

The following is a brief chronology of Clare's life around which I have built this story. This chronology and list of a few English texts may prove helpful to the reader who is unacquainted with the main events of her life.

1193 or 1194, Born in Assisi.

1199, Family moves to Perugia as a result of civil war in Assisi.

1205, Clare's family returns to Assisi.

1212, March 18/19, On Palm Sunday night, reception of Clare at the Portiuncula.

1212, March 19, The beginning of Clare's stay at San Paolo near Bastia.

1212, Soon after April 3, after a few days at San Paolo and a few weeks at Sant' Angelo di Panzo Benedictine convent, Clare moves to San Damiano.

1212, April 3/4, The entrance of Clare's sister Agnes.

1215, End, or beginning of 1216, Clare becomes abbess.

1215, December-July 26, 1216, The Privilege of Poverty of Innocent III.

1218, August 27, 1216, to July 29, 1219, The Rule of Hugolino.

1219, Clare's sister Agnes is sent as abbess to Monticelli near Florence.

1224-1225, The beginning of the severe, long illness of Clare.

1226 (about), The entrance of Clare's mother Ortolana.

1226, September to the beginning of October, Francis sends his last legacy to Clare and her sisters.

1226, October 4, The body of Francis is brought to San Damiano on the way to burial.

1227, March 19, Cardinal Hugolino becomes Pope Gregory IX.

1228, September 17, Gregory IX renews the Privilege of Poverty.

1229 (about), The entrance of Clare's sister Beatrice.

1234, Before June, the first letter of Clare to Agnes of Prague.

1235, The second letter of Clare to Agnes of Prague.

1238, The third letter of Clare to Agnes of Prague.

1240, September, The repelling of the Saracens.

1247, After August 6, Clare begins work on her own rule.

1250, June 6, With the Bull "Inter Personas" Pope Innocent lifts the universal obligation to observe his rule.

1250, About November 11, Clare is sick to the peril of her life.

1252, September 8, Cardinal Rainaldo visits Clare, who petitions him for the approval of her Rule.

1252, September 16, The Rule of Clare is approved through the Cardinal Protector, Rainaldo.

1252, December 25, In a marvelous manner Clare joins with the friars at San Francesco to experience the divine services.

1253, The Testament of Clare.

1253, Beginning, Clare's sister Agnes returns to San Damiano.

1253, April 27, Pope Innocent IV arrives in Assisi.

1253, Soon after April 27, he visits Clare for the first time.

1253, A few days before August 11, he visits Clare the second time.

1253, August 8, Clare's vision of the King of Glory. In the evening, Sister Benvenuta sees a vision of the Mother of God with the heavenly court at the deathbed of Clare.

1253, August 9, Pope Innocent IV approves the Rule of Clare with the Bull, "Solet Annuere."

1253, August 10, A friar brings the bull of approval to Clare from Perugia.

1253, August 11, Clare dies at San Damiano.

1253, August 12, Clare is buried in the church of San Giorgio in Assisi.

1253, October 18, Pope Innocent IV commissions Bishop Bartholomew of Spoleto to conduct the inquiry into the life and miracles of Clare by the Bull, "Gloriosus Deus."

1253, November 24-29, Testimony of the witnesses is taken for the process of canonization in the Monastery of San Damiano and in the church of San Paolo in Assisi.

1255, August 15, Saint Clare is canonized by Pope Alexander at Agnani.

1260, Saint Clare's body is transferred to Santa Chiara.

FURTHER READING AND LISTENING

Bodo, Murray, O.F.M. *A Mosaic of Francis: Making His Way Our Own* (audiocassette). Cincinnati, Ohio: St. Anthony Messenger Press, 1986.

—. *Francis: The Journey and The Dream*. Revised Edition. Cincinnati, Ohio: St. Anthony Messenger Press, 1988.

—. *Song of the Sparrow: Meditations and Poems to Pray By*. Cincinnati, Ohio: St. Anthony Messenger Press, 1976.

—. *Tales of St. Francis: Ancient Stories for Contemporary Living*. New York, N.Y.: Doubleday, 1988.

Bodo, Murray, O.F.M., and Saint Sing, Susan. *Seasons: Meditations and Songs for Lent and Advent in the Spirit of St. Francis* (audiocassette). Cincinnati, Ohio: St. Anthony Messenger Press, 1981.

Clare of Assisi: Early Documents, ed. and trans. Regis Armstrong, O.F.M. Cap. New York, N.Y.: Paulist Press, 1988.

de Robeck, Nesta. *Saint Clare of Assisi*. Chicago, Ill.: Franciscan Herald Press, 1980.

Dreyer, Elizabeth, Ph.D., Regis Armstrong, O.F.M. Cap., and Mary Francis Hone, O.S.C., *Clare of Assisi: A Woman for All Times* (audiocassette). Cincinnati, Ohio: St. Anthony Messenger Press, 1992.

Francis and Clare: The Complete Works, ed. and trans. Regis Armstrong, O.F.M. Cap., and Ignatius C. Brady, O.F.M. New York, N.Y.: Paulist Press, 1982.

Roggen, Heribert. *The Spirit of St. Clare*. Chicago, Ill.: Franciscan Herald Press, 1971.

Seraphim, Mary, P.C.P.A. *Clare: Her Light and Her Song*. Chicago, Ill.: Franciscan Herald Press, 1984.